Locomotives of the Rio Grande

Steam Roster compiled by
Cornelius W. Hauck and
Robert W. Richardson

Colorado Railroad Historical Foundation, Inc.

The Foundation is a non-profit Colorado institution organized to operate and perpetuate the Colorado Railroad Museum. The Museum was established in 1958 by Robert W. Richardson and Cornelius Hauck, for the preservation of Colorado's unique railroad heritage. Your support in the work of the Foundation and Museum is earnestly solicited; an inquiry will bring membership information.

Table of Contents

Colorado Railroad Historical Foundation
P. O. Box 10
Golden, Colo. 80401

Rio Grande Southern R.R. Silver San Juan Scenic Line

Title page—With a volcano-like eruption from its stack, simple articulated 2-8-8-2 No. 3617 assists 4-8-4 No. 1804 in getting the eastbound Royal Gorge out of Minturn, Colorado, on September 1, 1949. The 3600's were noted for their smoke producing ability. (Ross Grenard)

Front cover—The sub-zero stillness of a moonlit Rocky Mountain winter's night is shattered by a mighty Rio Grande articulated as she struggles up the three percent grade on the west side of Tennessee Pass, Colorado. Two more engines are spaced back in the train to lend their assistance in this scene that could be from anytime during the 1930's or 1940's. (From an original painting by Howard Fogg, courtesy of Leanin' Tree Publishing Company)

Back cover—The classic sound of General Motors 567 series engines reverberates from the walls of Coal Creek Canon as the Rio Grande's famous set of F9's leads the Rio Grande Zephyr around the curve into Tunnel No. 1 of the Moffat line west of Denver, on the first leg of the long trek across Colorado and Utah to the Mormon capital. (Ronald C. Hill)

Revised Edition—1983

PUBLISHED AND DISTRIBUTED BY THE COLORADO RAILROAD MUSEUM, Box 10, Golden, CO 80401.

Colorado Railroad Museum, Golden, Colorado
Locomotives of the Rio Grande
Bibliography: p.
1. Locomotives—United States. 2. Denver and Rio Grande Western Railroad. I. Title.
TJ603.2.C65 1980 625.2'6'0978 80-24685
ISBN 0-918654-25-4

Printed by
JOHNSON PUBLISHING COMPANY
Boulder, Colorado

Layout by Kenton Forrest
Captions by Charles Albi

Colorado Railroad Museum
BOX 10.
GOLDEN COLO. 80401

Locomotives of the Rio Grande

A Detailed Locomotive Roster of The Rio Grande System 1871 - 1983

PREFACE

The appearance of many handsome volumes in recent years dealing with the Rio Grande Railroad, in some 1,000 pages of text and illustration, might presumably have thoroughly covered the subject.

However, none of these works offer a detailed accounting of perhaps the single most significant physical property of the railroad: its motive power. To the serious railroad enthusiast or historian, such data is important — and has not been provided. A roster of locomotives had been published by the Railway and Locomotive Historical Society in 1949, in its Bulletin No. 77, but this publication is now out of print and unavailable.

To fill this need the Museum in 1963 had undertaken the job of publishing a roster of Rio Grande steam locomotives from 1871 to date. The roster was made as accurate and complete as possible, although in any such work there is inevitably room for corrections and additions. Thus in 1976, the Museum decided to update the roster and include the diesels of the Rio Grande. After many years of gathering facts and photos, the Museum is proud to present this updated locomotive roster of the Denver & Rio Grande Western Railroad.

We have consciously deleted the D&RG's first switch engine, for lack of accurate data as to weight, tractive effort or even gauge — for it was established, according to an exchange of letters in 1917 between E.A. Greenwood, stationed at Salt Lake City, and F.A. Wadleigh at Denver, that the 19th and Wewatta Street yards in Denver were switched during 1872 by a "large gray mule".

In preparing this roster, we have been influenced considerably by the R&LHS roster which preceded our original one by some 14 years, and seasoned railfans will note a marked similarity in format — a very practical arrangement which it seemed logical to follow. In our efforts we have had the encouragement and considerable help in the first roster by the late Charles E. Fisher of the Society, for which we are very grateful.

The basis for our data was largely an accumulation of material in Museum files, which included a copy of the Denver & Rio Grande 1880 locomotive record book, the original of which is now in the Division of State Archives and Public Records of Colorado; Rio Grande folio books of different years, Rio Grande Southern Railroad records and other materials.

Much added data was gathered from many sources. Museum volunteers such as Michael B. Davis and the late Kenneth C. Crist spent many hours in Denver and Salt Lake City unearthing elusive bits of data from dusty files. They also researched and assembled the data for the Rio Grande Western roster. Through the good offices of G.B. Aydelott, Chairman, Rio Grande Industries, certain needed data was obtained from official railroad files.

There were many people who did considerable research and gave valuable assistance. They include George B. Abdill, Albert Farrow, Bruce Black, P. Allen Copeland, Doug Cummings, Harold L. Goldsmith, the late Everett L. DeGolyer, Jr., Henry R. Griffiths, Joseph Harris, George W. Hilton, Carl E. Mulvihill, Jackson C. Thode, John A. Rehor, Frank Robinson, Dr. S.R. Wood, Harold Vollrath and Richard Will.

Others assisting with data and corrections were Col. Homer Benton, James J. Buckley, John Buvinger, Don Dover, Guy L. Dunscomb, Edward T. Francis, Richard H. Kindig, Louis R. Koeppe, Loring M. Lawrence, Robert A. Le Massena, Dirk P. Ramsey, D.S. Richter, Kent Stephens, F.H. Wagner, Jr., Tom Vesey, and the staffs of *Extra 2200 South, New Mexico Railroad Magazine* and *Trains Magazine*.

For the use of photographs, special thanks are due to Harold Vollrath; the State Historical Society of Colorado; the Denver Public Library Western History Department and A.D. Mastrogiuseppe; H.L. Broadbelt; Edward Fulcomer; John W. Maxwell; Fred M. Mazzulla; the History Center, City of Schenectady; Ross Grenard, and Ronald C. Hill.

The greatest credit is given to Cornelius W. Hauck and Robert W. Richardson, who over twenty years ago started the Colorado Railroad Museum at Golden and without whose work, time and money, none of this would have been possible.

The Trustees of the
Colorado Railroad Historical Foundation
Golden, Colorado

All three cylinders of 4-8-2 No. 1601 are clearly visible in this view about October 1927, at Salida. The size of the huge locomotive is emphasized by comparison with the men working on her. (H.E. High photo, Richard H. Kindig Collection)

STEAM LOCOMOTIVE DEVELOPMENT ON THE RIO GRANDE

The narrow gauge Denver & Rio Grande that struggled south from Denver in 1871 — intended for El Paso — bore little relation physically to today's Rio Grande — or even to the least pretentious narrow gauge Rio Grande branches of recent years. Grading was minimal and ballast non-existant; ties rough-cut and untreated, and tie plates unheard-of; the 30 lb. iron rail was the equivalent of that used for light mine service today.

Over this primitive track only the lightest of equipment could be used. Between 1871 and 1873 the D&RG acquired 12 new locomotives from the Baldwin Locomotive Works, which constituted the Road's entire roster. Four were very light (12½ tons) 2-4-0 type for passenger service, and eight were somewhat larger moguls of 17½ tons, for freight service. In 1876-78 a number of slightly larger moguls and some eightwheelers were added from Baldwin, and while these too were very light they did present an improvement over the original designs.

The initial Rio Grande construction from Denver to Pueblo involved no real mountain railroading, no severe grades. In 1876, however, a line was begun from Cucharas (near Walsenburg) over Veta Pass, into the San Luis Valley, that contained all the features of a true mountain narrow gauge, including long 4% grades and 30° curves. The difficult operating requirements of this line dictated more powerful locomotives, light track not withstanding.

To provide an answer, Baldwin in 1877 produced what was to become the "standard motive power" for the narrow gauge for decades to come — the D&RG's first 2-8-0, the "Alamosa". At 34 tons it was nearly twice the weight of the original moguls, and would do more than twice the work, yet it was still able to successfully negotiate the Rio Grande's fragile trackwork.

During the five years from 1877 through 1881 — the period of the D&RG's tremendous expansion through the mountains to the booming gold and silver camps, and to Salt Lake — the road purchased over 150 of these little consolidations, from Baldwin and Grant. They were produced in two sizes: Class 56, with 15x18″ cylinders, and slightly larger Class 60, with 15x20″ cylinders. Still larger were the 400s, later numbered 340-349, but they were confined in early years to use on the heavy grades of Marshall Pass, where track and rail were sufficiently sturdy to support them.

Other narrow gauge power purchased in the eighties included eightwheelers and tenwheelers for passenger use; none, however, larger than the Class 60 engines. The decision to standard gauge the entire Denver-Ogden line in 1887 effectively ended purchases of narrow gauge locomotives. After 1888 there was a tremendous surplus of narrow gauge power on the D&RG, due both to the standard gauging and the recession in mining. Older, lighter engines were sold in great numbers in the early nineties. Many Class 56 and 60 engines were sold to the new Rio Grande Southern, from both the D&RG and the Rio Grande Western. Moguls and eightwheelers were sold to lumber and mill roads throughout Texas and the south, with some going to such faraway places as Pennsylvania, Florida and Mexico.

First to go in the narrow-gauge locomotive housecleaning were the original 18 small locomotives of 1871-1876, and the light moguls. Most of these were sold or dismantled in the 1888-1890 period. The newer and larger eightwheelers (of which 19 were on the roster in 1890) were largely displaced by tenwheelers on the remaining through narrow gauge passenger trains, and were gradually sold. Ten went in the 1891-1894 period alone, and only four were still on the roster by 1900 — nos. 85, 94, 96 and 100 (the latter not being scrapped until 1908). Their use in later years was confined to a few light runs such as the La Veta-Creede day accommodation, official or special trains, work trains, and occasional duty as switchers.

By the turn of the century, Colorado and the Rio Grande's traffic had recovered somewhat from the effects of the Silver Crash of 1893. The 32 miles of 4% grade over Marshall Pass, where the heaviest C-19 or 70 Class were assigned, was a particularly difficult stretch with heavy trains, and in 1903 the

Rio Grande purchased 15 new engines from Baldwin for this Salida-Sargent run. The new engines, #450-464, were "huge" outside frame Vauclain compound 2-8-2's, and they could haul double the load up the "hill" of the old 70 Class engines. The latter were then shifted to Cumbres Pass, where a rail replacement program enabled them to work as far west as Chama.

Of the 2-8-0s, Class 60 engines were preferred to the lighter Class 56, and the latter were eliminated from the roster by gradual attrition. Eleven were transferred to the D&RGW Ry (Utah) in 1886, and a half dozen were sold at varying times. Following acquisition of the 15 Class K-27 engines in 1903, and standard gauging of the La Veta-Creede, Grand Junction-Montrose and North Fork lines in the 1900-1906 period, the Rio Grande had a large surplus of small narrow gauge power. As a result, 25 Class 56 engines were dismantled in 1908. With new, stringent ICC boiler requirements in 1916, the remaining 9 engines in the class were deemed unworthy of upgrading and were scrapped.

By 1914 a few Class 125 2-8-2s (termed "mudhens") were operating out of Chama on Cumbres Hill, but light rail and poor track prevented their use on other stretches of the Alamosa-Durango line until after 1920, when a major rail-relaying program was carried out. The heavier 2-8-0s were still in active use on main line trains, often doubleheading with 2-8-2s on Cumbres and Marshall Pass. In 1916-1920 the D&RG acquired nine additional relatively modern 2-8-0s second hand from other defunct Colorado railroads. Six came from the Florence & Cripple Creek — Baldwins of 1895-1897, which formed Class C-18; originally numbered 424-429, they were later renumbered 315-320, and two still survive (no. 315 at Durango, and 318, in operating condition, at the Colorado Railroad Museum). The other three were from the Crystal River RR and were the only outside-frame 2-8-0s on the D&RG — two (Baldwin 1900) became Class C-21 and saw many years' use (as nos. 360 and 361) on the Black Canyon line; the third was nearly as powerful as a K-27 and became the sole engine in Class C-25 (Baldwin 1903; no. 432, later 375).

With the system-wide track upgrading of the early twenties came the opportunity to utilize newer, heavier power over much of the narrow gauge. First to be acquired were 10 new Class K-28 2-8-2s from Alco, nos. 470-479. Only modestly heavier than a K-27, they were much faster and more efficient, and soon became favored for the remaining passenger runs, as well as freight, thus displacing the old Class T-12 tenwheelers. Six Class T-12s were scrapped in 1926, and four more in 1934-1937, with two being donated for preservation (no. 168 at Colorado Springs, and 169 at Alamosa). Seven of the handsome and popular K-28s (sometimes called "sports models") had their own careers on the Rio Grande cut short in 1942, when they were requisitioned by the U.S. Army for use on the White Pass & Yukon Route in Alaska.

Another ten 2-8-2s arrived from Baldwin in 1925, and these Class K-36 freight haulers were fully ⅓ more powerful than the old K-27s. Finally, in 1928-1930, Burnham Shops rebuilt ten old standard gauge 2-8-0s (Class C-41, Baldwin 1902) into new narrow gauge 2-8-2s of Class K-37, the largest yet. These twenty locomotives were the mainstay of freight service on the Gunnison and Alamosa-Farmington lines for the remaining years of operation. Initially the K-37s were used on the Gunnison lines and the K-36s west of Alamosa, but in later years, as traffic patterns shifted, five of the K-37s were exchanged with K-36s for service over Cumbres, where they could handle one additional car more.

In final years, a few 2-8-0s continued in service on the Crested Butte, Baldwin, Black Canyon and Ouray lines, where light track or bridge clearances limited locomotive size, or as switchers. The K-27s were seen on the Montrose lines, on lease to the Rio Grande Southern, or on Durango-Silverton-Farmington trains until displaced by 470s.

Standard gauge motive power development at first closely paralleled that of the narrow gauge. The first standard gauge trackage, in 1882, was merely a third rail laid on the existing 3′ gauge line from Denver to Pueblo, and by necessity the engines bought from Baldwin for this service — 2-8-0s and 4-6-0s — were little different or heavier than their narrow gauge counterparts.

However, the coming of the standard gauge Colorado Midland in 1887 forced a radical change upon the D&RG. The main line was rehabilitated and relaid to standard gauge from Denver to Ogden between 1888 and 1890; heavier rail was used over the entire route, and a new line utilized over Tennessee Pass and through Glenwood Springs to avoid the difficult Marshall Pass-Black Canyon line.

To move freight efficiently over this new standard gauge route, the D&RG and RGW ordered, between 1888 and 1892, 118 consolidations of a standard design from Baldwin. These engines were modern, heavy power for their day, and in fact were the first locomotives to use the then-radical extended wagon-top boilers with radial stayed fireboxes. One of these original 2-8-0s, #583, is on exhibit at the Colorado Railroad Museum, and is the only standard gauge Rio Grande steam locomotive to have been preserved.

At the same time, the D&RG obtained 33 smart

tenwheelers from Baldwin for passenger service, and the RGW also acquired a number from Rome (New York Locomotive Works) and Baldwin.

Recovering from the 1893 Silver Crash, the Rio Grande relaid the Denver-Pueblo line with 85# rail, and began ordering more tenwheelers, heavy moguls and consolidations. 141 2-8-0s alone were added in the following decade, and most of these ranged from 90 to 110 tons — considerably more than the 60 tons of the Class C-28 engines of a decade previous.

The consolidations and tenwheelers continued to do the bulk of the work on the line for many years. The first articulateds were not purchased until 1910; 14 mikados came from Baldwin in 1912 and 10 2-10-2s from Brooks in 1917. Six new Pacifics from Baldwin in 1913 took over the premier passenger assignments.

During the 1920s, after the Road's reorganization as the Denver & Rio Grande Western, the Rio Grande began acquiring larger and more modern power. The old consolidations and tenwheelers soon gave way to big new 4-8-2s from Brooks and Baldwin; handsome 4-8-4s from Baldwin; and more articulateds from Richmond, Brooks and Schenectady. This completed the transformation of the Rio Grande's roster to modern power, with the exception of 15 4-6-6-4 simple articulateds added in 1938 and 1942, and 5 more 4-8-4s from Baldwin.

Down through the years, the Rio Grande had many more locomotives on hand than might have been expected for a road of its traffic level. Many of these locomotives were smaller, older power demoted from main line service. These engines often saw service for many years as helpers, or switching the many mine, mill and smelter spurs on the Rio Grande. They were very necessary in this service, but could see years of such service without accumulating much mileage or requiring very heavy maintenance.

Dieselization had begun when World War II, with its sudden crush of traffic, descended upon the Rio Grande. New diesels were in short supply; there was no answer but to try to obtain more steam power as well. Six "war baby" 4-6-6-4 articulateds were obtained from Schenectady in 1943; they were soon resold to the Clinchfield, who also used them briefly and then set them aside for scrap. 17 aging compound articulateds and 4 4-8-2s were obtained from the Norfolk & Western, products of Baldwin and the Roanoke Shops. The 4-8-2s were later sold to the Wheeling & Lake Erie, but the articulateds were worn out in service.

Generally, steam locomotive development on the Rio Grande system was quite orderly, and the Rio Grande roster does not reflect the vast assortment of motley, unrelated locomotives often noted on other roads. The reason is obvious — the Rio Grande's development was entirely internal, through construction of its own lines, whereas many other roads expanded through mergers and absorption of smaller lines — thus inheriting various assortments of motive power. Even the exceptions to this pattern often did not disturb the picture — as in the case of the purchase of the Florence & Cripple Creek engines in 1916, or the Norfolk & Western engines — where they formed distinct classes.

One major exception to the mergerless pattern was the absorption of the Denver & Salt Lake roster in 1947, in the twilight of standard gauge steam on the Rio Grande.

Between 1950 and 1955 steam was scrapped as quickly as it could be replaced. It is interesting to note what engines were still on hand by 1955, out of the many in service a decade earlier. All of the modern 1800s and most of the 3700s were gone, as were all the big 3-cylinder 4-8-2s. A few 1200-series 2-8-2s, 1400 2-10-2s, 1500 Brooks 4-8-2s, and big 1700s were on hand, along with a few ex-D&SL engines. The only Classes represented in any number were the big 3600 2-8-8-2s, all of which remained, along with some 35 lowly consolidations of the 1100 Class. One of these C-48 engines, #1151, made the final run of standard gauge steam on the Rio Grande on December 26, 1956, from Alamosa to South Fork and return; dismantling was begun the next day, and by December 31 the Rio Grande standard gauge was 100% diesel — after 85 years of steam operation.

The dainty and finely decorated 2-4-0 Montezuma, the first locomotive for the brand new Denver & Rio Grande Railway, is seen at the Baldwin Locomotive Works in Philadelphia in May 1871. Note improvised "track" laid over the cobble stones. (H.L. Broadbelt Collection)

KEY TO ROSTER

with Explanatory Notes

Locomotives are listed numerically (by road number), for the most part, with a few exceptions. This also yields a generally chronological listing as well. In addition, beginning with no. 150 the locomotives are grouped according to class. In looking up specific locomotives, bear in mind that many Rio Grande locomotives were renumbered at one time or another; for the most part, locomotives in this roster are listed under their original numbers.

Disposition of locomotives are shown, with subsequent resales where known. Dates of disposition, where engines were dismantled, are somewhat arbitrary; the dates given are generally those shown in D&RGW records, and may be the date on which the particular locomotive was entered in the records as "dismantled" rather than the actual date the torch cut the metal. In some cases, there is evidence to indicate a locomotive was sold after being listed as scrapped, for use on an operation not under ICC surveillance.

Specifications are uniformly listed in this order: cylinder dimensions; driver diameters; total engine weight; tractive effort (TE); boiler pressure (BP). Generally these are the specifications listed in Rio Grande folio books or other railroad sources. These may be at variance with original builders' specifications, and in fact there is great variance in the railroad's data. For as engines were shopped over the years, they gradually became rebuilt until specifications not only differed from earlier years but also differed between different engines in the same class.

Abbreviations are used in the listings to simplify the entries where possible. They are as follows:

Dism — Dismantled, or scrapped.

Sold to — Indicating change in ownership and physical possession, through outright sale.

To — Transfer, physically, without necessarily formal sale (as, D&RG engines transferred to D&RGW Ry ownership in 1886).

Then to — Subsequent change in status, generally through change in name of owning railroad, or reincorporation.

Later on — Indicating apparent sale or transfer, but not necessarily given in complete order.

Reno — Renumbered. Unless otherwise specified, this refers to the 1924 system renumbering.

Orig — Originally.

Ret — Retired or removed from service.

Disp — Disposition.

Rblt — Rebuilt.

From — Received from, through merger or other means.

D&RGW Ry — Denver & Rio Grande Western Railway, a Utah Corporation and predecessor of the Rio Grande Western, not to be confused with the later D&RGW (Denver & Rio Grande Western Railroad Company).

D&RG No. 3, the Shou-wa-no, was a Mogul type intended for freight service. (H.L. Broadbelt Collection)

CLASSIFICATION OF NARROW GAUGE ENGINES

NUMBERS 1 THROUGH 109

These first 109 D&RG locomotives were numbered in approximate chronological order, rather than by individual classes as was the case after 1880. Accordingly, these locomotives are listed here also in numerical order, with their class designation, and the specifications for each class are listed below. The following are the original specifications as indicated by early D&RG records.

CLASS	TYPE	CYLINDERS	DRIVERS	ENGINE WT.	TRACTIVE EFFORT
25	2-4-0	9x16″	40″	25,000#	3,580#
35	2-6-0	11x16″	36″	35,000#	5,940#
37	4-4-0	11x16″	44″	37,000#	4,750#
38	4-4-0	12x16″	45″	37,000#	5,660#
39	0-6-0T	11x16″	36″	39,000#	6,200#
40	2-6-0	12x16″	36″	40,000#	7,060#
40*	2-6-0	13¼x20″	38″	52,000#	
42	4-4-0	12x18″	45″	40,000#	6,380#
42½	4-4-0	12x18″	45″	44,150#	6,380#
48	0-6-0T	14x16″	36″	48,000#	9,640#
56	2-8-0	15x18″	36″	56,000#	12,450#
60	2-8-0	15x20″	36″	60,000#	13,800#

Note*: All orginal (Baldwin) Class 40 engines followed the first dimensions above. When the Santa Fe Southern moguls were acquired in 1895, all of the original Class 40 D&RG engines had been disposed of, and the SFS locomotives were assigned the Class designation 40. The second set of dimensions are for these latter locomotives.

All of the above locomotives were purchased new from the Baldwin Works, with the exception of the Santa Fe Southern engines.

Class 42½ differed from Class 42 in that the former were designed to burn anthracite coal, and operate out of Grand Juncton. They would not steam and were generally considered unsatisfactory.

The specifications of these locomotives became varied through rebuildings and shoppings — and there is some reason to question the accuracy of the original specifications as well. A folio book of about 1904 provides some different data on several of these Classes, as follows:

42	4-4-0	12x18″	46″	40,000#	6,646#
56	2-8-0	15x18″	37″	56,200#	13,025#
60	2-8-0	15x20″	37″	58,600#	14,989#

However, Class 60 engines of the same group, in service on the Rio Grande Southern, were rated in the same folio book with only 14,474# tractive effort.

1	#2459-1871	2-4-0	25	"Montezuma"; Put up for sale 10/87; Dism 7/23/88; Boiler to Salida Hospital; Destroyed by fire 4/12/99.
2	#2479-1871	2-6-0	35	"Tabi-wachi"; leased to H. R. W. Scott, Geist, Mather Bros. & Scott Co. (Mather & Geist — Pueblo Smelting & Refining Co.) 11/82-1/83; Rebuilt to 0-6-0T class 39 7/17/83; to A. T. Sullenberger & Co. 11/8/88 in exchange for #29, and renamed "Azotea"; Dism Burnham 8/31/98.
3	#2476-1871	2-6-0	35	"Shou-wa-no"; Rebuilt to 0-6-0T class 39 7/11/84; Sold to San Francisco Construction Co. 8/22/88; See #11.
4	#2566-1871	2-4-0	25	"Cortez"; Put up for sale 10/87; Dism 7/23/88; Boiler to Salida Hospital; Destroyed by fire 4/12/99.

5	#2568-1871	2-6-0	35	"Ouray"; Leased to H. D. Fisher & Co. 1880; Sold to W. T. Carpenter, Grand Junction, 11/12/89, as Little Book Cliff RR. #1.
6	#2613-1871	2-4-0	25	"Ute"; Leased to Denver, Longmont & Northwestern RR. 1881-84; Sold 11/10/86 to Denver Railroad Land & Coal Co., then (1/88) Colorado Eastern, #6; At Morse Bros., Denver, on 8/22/15; Perhaps to Leadville smelter.
7	#2617-1871	2-4-0	25	"Del Norte"; Leased to Denver Circle RR. 10/25/82-8/13/83; Put up for sale 10/87; Dism 11/88.
8	#2727-1871	2-6-0	35	"Arkansas"; Leased to Denver, Longmont & Northwestern RR. 1881-84; Rebuilt to 0-6-0T class 39 1/31/84; Sold to Arkansas Valley Smelter (American Smelting & Refining Co.) 7/10/88.
9	#2728-1871	2-6-0	35	"Huerfano"; to Mather & Geist under lease 1882 and 12/83; Dism 3/23/88.
10	#2897-1873	2-6-0	35	"San Carlos"; Leased to Denver, Longmont & Northwestern and Denver, Utah & Pacific RRs. 1882-87; Put up for sale 10/87; Dism 3/23/88.
11	#3021-1873	2-6-0	35	"Cucharas"; Leased to Denver, Longmont & Northwestern RR. 1882-84; Rebuilt to 0-6-0T class 39 3/23/85; Sold to San Francisco Construction Co. 6/5/88.
				Note: Nos. 3 and 11 were used on construction work in the San Francisco area, and then were reported to have gone to the firm's installation at Adoth, Nevada, where one was reported still in service in 1904, when it was replaced by a new Vulcan. No. 11 may have gone to a lumber operation in the Coos Bay, Oregon, area, while no. 3 may have become Terry Lumber Co. no. 3. In addition, a light 0-6-0T said to be ex-Rio Grande was reported at Pioche (Pioche Consolidated Mining & Reduction Co., later Pioche Pacific RR. of the Nevada-Utah Mining & Smelting Co.) in the 1891-1908 period.
12	#3165-1873	2-6-0	35	"Las Animas"; Leased to Mather & Geist 9/83-12/83; Rebuilt to 0-6-0T class 39 3/17/84; Sold to Alfred C. Torbett, 6/99.
13	Vulcan	0-4-4-0T		See #101.
13	#3806-1876	2-6-0	40	"Santa Clara"; Dism 7/1/89. This engine not to be confused with "Mosca" #13 2-8-0 built for D&RG, but not placed in service acc. too heavy for track (see #24 below).
14	#3809-1876	2-6-0	40	"Chicosa"; Sold 1/92 to G. M. Dilley & Son, Palestine, Tex., for $2,000 less $100 for repairs; later on Josserand Lumber; then West Lumber.
15	#3810-1876	2-6-0	40	"Raton"; Sold 5/22/91 to G. M. Dilley & Son for $2,000 less 10% commission; May have become New Mexico Lumber Company's (1st)#2, 11/95.
16	#3867-1876	4-4-0	37	"Pike"; For sale 10/87; Dism Burnham 6/19/88.
17	#3869-1876	4-4-0	37	"Greenhorn"; Sold to R. W. Stewart & Co. 10/31/88.
18	#3871-1876	4-4-0	37	"Spanish Peaks"; For sale 10/87; Dism Burnham 6/19/88.
19	#3899-1876	2-6-0	40	"Sangre de Cristo"; Built for Philadelphia Centennial Exposition Railway as "Delaware"; Sold to Arkansas Valley Smelter, Leadville, 4/25/99.
20	#4057-1877	0-6-0T	48	Sold to Mike Elmore, 5/00.

21	#4058-1877	0-6-0T	48	Sold to Streeter & Kennefick, Chicago, 9/6/93 for $1,600.
22	#4076-1877	2-8-0	60	"Alamosa"; Reno. 228 at Burnham, 11/30/94; Dism 3/26.
23	#4158-1877	2-6-0	40	"Trinchera"; Sold to LaPlata Constr. Co. and returned, 6/91; Sold to Biggs Lumber Co. 12/95 for $2,000, as Tierra Amarilla Southern #2; Later on Rio Grande & Pagosa Springs RR of New Mexico Lumber Co. as #3; Then Pagosa Lumber Co. #2.
24	#4191-1877	2-8-0	56	"Mosca"; Reno. 41 at Burnham 11/30/94; Dism. Note: Not to be confused with a #13 "Mosca," a 2-8-0 built by Baldwin in 1873 allegedly for the D&RG, but not delivered and sold to the East Broad Top RR & Coal Co.
24	#424-1880 Pittsburgh Loco. Works	2-6-0	40	Orig. Cairo & St. Louis RR #26; Then Santa Fe Southern #4; To D&RG 2nd #24 in 1895; Dropped from Equipment (6/99?) and Dism.
25	#4192-1878	2-8-0	56	"Hardscrabble"; Reno. 42 at Burnham 1/31/95; Dism 6/30/08.
25	#423-1880 Pittsburgh Loco. Works	2-6-0	40	Orig. Cairo & St. Louis RR #27; Then Santa Fe Southern #5; To D&RG 2nd #25 in 1895; Dropped from Equipment (6/99?) and Dism.
26	#4331-1878	4-4-0	38	"Rio Bravo"; Dism Burnham 8/31/98.
27	#4317-1878	2-6-0	40	"Poncha"; Sold to Sabine Tramway Co., Orange, Texas, for $1,600 on 3/8/89 (?).
28	#4335-1878	2-6-0	40	"Nepesta"; Sold to George Laws, 11/3/90, for $2,000, as Tierra Amarilla Southern #1.
29	#4336-1878	2-6-0	40	"Cochetope"; Sold 1888 to A. T. Sullenberger; Exchanged 11/8/88 for #2; Sold to Rio Grande Southern RR #11, 1/6/91; to Geo. M. Dilley & Son 1899; to Yellow Pine Lumber Co.
30	#4382-1878	2-8-0	56	"Old Baldy"; Leased to Denver, South Park & Pacific RR 7/79 to 1/80; Dism 6/30/16.
31	#4384-1878	2-8-0	56	"Dolores"; Rebuilt to 0-8-0; Dism 2/28/17.
32	#4385-1878	2-8-0	56	"Kit Carson"; Leased to Denver, South Park & Pacific RR 7/79 to 1/80; to Pueblo Steel Works 9/28/82 to 2/22/84; and to Florence & Cripple Creek RR during 2/94; Dism 6/30/08.
33	#4504-1879	2-8-0	56	"Silver Cliff"; Dism 6/30/08.
34	#4505-1879	2-8-0	56	"Royal Gorge"; Dism 2/28/17.
35	#4738-1879	4-4-0	38	"Culebra"; Leased to Denver & Rio Grande Western Ry 11/7/87, returned 9/13/88; Sold to Geo. M. Dilley & Son 2/8/93 for $2,000; Later on Bering Mfg. Co. railroad.
36	#4825-1879	4-4-0	38	"San Juan"; Sold to Geo. M. Dilley & Son 8/93 for $2,200; Later on Cameron Lumber Mills Co. railroad.
37	#4809-1879	2-8-0	56	"Piedra"; Sold 6/07 to Pagosa Lumber Co.
38	#4811-1879	2-8-0	56	"Mancos"; Leased to Silverton RR 1/24/90; Dism 6/30/08.
39	#4871-1879	2-8-0	56	"Chama"; Retired 6/03; Dism 6/30/08.
40	#4872-1879	2-8-0	56	"Elk Mountain"; Sold to Halleck & Howard Lumber Co. 2/28/17.
41	#4940-1880	2-8-0	60	"Grand Canyon"; Reno. 229 at Salida 7/2/84; Dism 1936.
41	#4191-1877			2nd #41, ex #24. See that number.
42	#4938-1880	2-8-0	60	"Anglo Saxon"; Sold to Silverton RR #100 11/2/87 for $6,500; Dism on S.RR 1909-12; See Note after #283.

42	#4192-1878			2nd #42, ex #25. See that number.
43	#4942-1880	2-8-0	56	"Copper Gulch"; Dism 6/30/08.
44	#4974-1880	2-8-0	56	"Texas Creek"; Sold to North Shore RR #40 6/03 for $4,000; To Northwestern Pacific #321; Dism 12/31/10.
45	#4976-1880	2-8-0	56	"Mojanda"; Dism 6/30/08.
46	#4981-1880	2-8-0	56	"Badito"; Sold to New Mexico Lumber Co. (2nd)#2 4/03, $5,000; in use on their Rio Grande & Pagosa Springs RR and Rio Grande & Southwestern RR.
47	#4985-1880	2-8-0	56	"Gold Town"; Rented to Pueblo Smelting & Refining Co. 2/93; Dism 6/30/08.
48	#4984-1880	2-8-0	56	"Current Creek"; Leased to Rio Grande Southern RR, Durango, 1/92, returned 2/92; Dism 6/30/08.
49	#4986-1880	2-8-0	56	"Badger"; To Burns & Biggs Lumber Co., Brazos Road, returned 8/21/02; Dism 6/30/08.
50	#4992-1880	2-8-0	56	"Crestones"; Leased to Rio Grande Southern RR 1/13/92, returned 2/10/92; Rebuilt to 0-8-0; Dism 2/28/17.
51	#4990-1880	2-8-0	56	"South Arkansas"; Either Dism 6/30/08 or sold to Azucarera de Altimira.
52	#5002-1880	2-8-0	56	"Music Pass"; Dism 6/30/08.
53	#5006-1880	2-8-0	56	"Cottonwood"; Transferred to "Rio Grande Gunnison RR" 12/26/91, returned 1/2/92; Dism 6/30/08.
54	#5008-1880	2-8-0	56	"Ruby Camp"; Dism 6/30/08.
55	#5011-1880	2-8-0	56	"Tomichi"; Leased to Silverton RR 8/91-11/91; Sold to Uintah RR 5/23/04 for $3,000 and reno. 11; Dism 1911.
56	#5018-1880	2-8-0	56	"Buffalo Peaks"; Sold to Sayer-Newton Lumber Co. 11/02 for $5,000; Later A. A. Rust; Then Hallack & Howard Lbr. Co. #1.
57	#5021-1880	2-8-0	56	"Chalk Creek"; Dism 6/30/08.
58	#5022-1880	2-8-0	56	"Fryer Hill"; Rebuilt to 0-8-0; Dism 2/28/17.
59	#5023-1880	2-8-0	56	"Hoosier"; Dism 6/30/08.
60	#5039-1880	2-8-0	56	"Mosquito Gulch"; Dism 6/30/08.
61	#5040-1880	2-8-0	56	"La Jara"; Leased to Silverton RR 10 and 11/90; Dism 6/30/08.
62	#5041-1880	2-8-0	56	"San Antonio"; Dism 6/30/08.
63	#5051-1880	2-8-0	56	"Mt. Agassiz"; Dism 6/30/08.
64	#5069-1880	2-8-0	56	"Tres Piedras"; Rebuilt to 0-8-0; Dism 6/30/16.
65	#5096-1880	2-8-0	56	"San Cristoval"; Leased to Silverton RR 1/1/90, returned 1/23/90; Rebuilt to 0-8-0; Dism 2/28/17.
66	#5098-1880	2-8-0	56	"Bristol Head"; Leased to Pueblo Steel Works 2/22/84, returned 10/1/84; Leased to Biggs Lumber Co. 11/17/92, returned 12/23/92; Dism 6/30/08.
67	#5102-1880	2-8-0	56	"Weminuche"; Leased to Silverton RR 10 and 11/90; Dism 6/30/08.
68	#5103-1880	2-8-0	56	"Vermejo"; Dism 6/30/08.
69	#5132-1880	2-8-0	56	"Arroya Honda"; Dism 6/30/08.
70	#5133-1880	2-8-0	56	"Sierra Madre"; Sold 4/07 to Pagosa Lumber Co.

71	#5136-1880	2-8-0	56	"Pacific Slope"; Sold to Denver & Rio Grande Western Ry #71 7/12/86, then Rio Grande Western #71; Sold to Rio Grande Southern RR #27, 1891; Sold to Carolina & Northwestern #230, 9/27/99; Sold to Gainesville, Jefferson & Southern, then Gainesville Midland (on hand 11/08). See RGS #27.
71		2-8-0	56	Ex Santa Fe Southern #3 to D&RG 2nd #71 on 11/11/95; class assignment may have been arbitrary; Dism 6/30/08.
72	#5137-1880	2-8-0	56	"Piedra"; Sold to D&RGW Ry #72 7/12/86; then RGW #72; Sold to RGS #28, 1891; Sold to Detroit Copper Mining Co. #10, then to Morenci Southern Ry #1, 1900.
73	#5138-1880	2-8-0	56	"Sneffels"; Sold to D&RGW Ry #73 7/12/86; then RGW #73; Sold to RGS #29, 1891; Sold to Detroit Copper Mining Co. #...., then to Morenci Southern Ry #2, 1900.
74	#5164-1880	2-8-0	56	"Hermano"; Sold to D&RGW Ry #74 7/12/86; then RGW #74; Sold to RGS #30, 1891; Sold to RGW #04, 1899; Sold to Sumpter Valley RR #7, 1900, then #10; out of service 1924; Dism ca. 1936.
75	#5166-1880	2-8-0	56	"Uncompahgre"; Sold to D&RGW Ry #75 7/12/86; then RGW #75; Rebuilt to SG and Reno. 2; Dism 1902-03.
76	#5184-1880	2-8-0	56	"U.S. Mountain"; Sold to D&RGW Ry #76 7/12/86, then RGW #76; Sold to RGS #31, 1891; Sold to Detroit Copper Mining Co. #11, then to Morenci Southern #3, 1900; Later on Franklin & Abbeville RR; Nacozari RR.
77	#5185-1880	2-8-0	56	"Rinconida"; Sold to D&RGW Ry #77 7/12/86, then RGW #77; Sold to RGS #32, 1891; Sold to Silverton Gladstone & Northerly #32, 1899; Dism about 1909-12; Boiler ab. at Teffts Spur.
78	#5225-1880	2-8-0	56	"Sandia"; Sold to D&RGW Ry #78 7/12/86, then RGW #78; Sold to RGS #33, 1891; Sold to Geo. M. Dilley & Son, 1899. Note: This locomotive was reported returned by Dilley in 1901, sold to SG&N #33 in 1902, and dismantled about 1903. However, a notation in Baldwin records indicates an "R. G. Brown" as later owner; thus the report on SG&N is inaccurate, or the boiler for this engine was perhaps exchanged for that of another class 56 engine during shopping by the D&RG, resulting in a misleading entry in Baldwin records based on the construction number on the builder plate.
79	#5226-1880	2-8-0	56	"La Plata"; Sold to D&RGW Ry #79 7/12/86, then RGW #79; Sold to RGS #34, 1891; Sold to Silverton RR #101, 1892, then Silverton Northern #1, 1896; Dism about 1920.
80	#5200-1880	2-8-0	56	"Chico"; Sold to D&RGW Ry #80 7/12/86, then RGW #80; Sold to RGS #35, 1891; Sold to Boston Coal & Fuel Co. (Calumet Fuel Co.) #1, 1901; Became RGS (2nd) #1, 1906; Dism 1913.
81	#5373-1880	2-8-0	56	"Puerco"; Sold to D&RGW Ry #81 7/12/86, then RGW #70; Later on Robinson Land & Lumber railroad.
82	#5374-1880	2-8-0	56	"Colo-Chiquito"; Dism 6/30/08.
83	#5423-1881	2-8-0	56	"Sera La Sal"; Dism 6/30/16.
84	#5156-1880	2-8-0	56	"Bill Williams"; Leased to Rio Grande Southern RR. 12/28/90-2/13/91; Leased to Rio Grande Gunnison RR 12/9/91-12/26/91; May have been sold to Santa Fe Southern RR 10/8/93; Off roster.
85	#4948-1880	4-4-0	42	"Fort De Remer"; Sold to Gurdon Lumber Co., Gurdon, Ark., 1/15/00 for $2,000; Later on Morris Lumber Co. and St. Louis Refrigerator & Wooden Gutter Co. railroads.

86	#5042-1880	4-4-0	42	"San Miguel"; Sold to F. C. Torres a Prietas, 7/31/96 for $1,800, and later (as of 9/10) Union Mexicano; Dism.
87	#5053-1880	4-4-0	42	"Rito Alto"; Sold 12/94 to Sanford & St. Petersburg RR, #11; Later on Flint River L. & E. Co. railroad.
88	#5198-1880	4-4-0	42	"Ptarmigan"; Sold to Carmen Island Salt Co. 5/6/92 for $2,000; Later on F. C. Torres a Prietas, which became Union Mexicano; Dism.
89	#5105-1880	4-4-0	38	"Eagle River"; Sold 8/1/93 to Geo. M. Dilley & Son, returned 12/95; Sold to Mike Elmore, 5/00.
90	#5106-1880	4-4-0	38	"Wahsatch"; Leased to AT&SF RR 9/26/89, returned 12/89; Either dismantled at Alamosa 8/31/98 or (from Baldwin records) sold to R. E. Trabue.
91	#5107-1880	4-4-0	38	"Ten Mile"; Sold to Geo. M. Dilley & Son 8/1/93; Later on Teche RR & Lumber Co., and R. E. Trabue.
92	#5118-1880	4-4-0	42	"Mogollon"; Sold to Sanford & St. Petersburg #12, 12/94; Then Atlantic Coast Line RR #801, #1801 (9/3/11); Later (4/4/12) on Sanford Mfg. Co. railroad.
93	#5119-1880	4-4-0	42	"Roaring Forks"; Sold to Rio Grande Southern RR #36, 11/27/91, for $1,000; Sold to Arkansas Lumber Co.
94	#5139-1880	4-4-0	42	"Gunnison"; Retired 6/03.
95	#5140-1880	4-4-0	42	"Embuda"; Sold to Sanford & St. Petersburg RR #5, 1/19/94, for $1,900; Then Atlantic Coast Line RR #800; Later (5/1/08) Georgia Car & Locomotive Works #41, and converted to standard gauge; To Lutz & Vincent #99, 8/28/11.
96	#5144-1880	4-4-0	42	"Morena"; Retired 6/03.
97	#5088-1880	0-6-0T	48	Leased to Pueblo Smelting & Refining Co., 8/11/85 and 7/8/86; Sold to Colorado & Kansas City Smelting & Refining Co. 2/7/93 for $3,600; Later Arkansas Valley Smelter, American Smelting & Refining Co., #3.
98	#5090-1880	0-6-0T	48	Sold to Streeter & Kennefick, Chicago, 9/93 for $1,900.
99	#5425-1881	4-4-0	42	"Kokomo"; Sold to Sanford & St. Petersburg RR 1/19/94; Later (1/98) on Flint River Lumber railroad.
100	#5436-1881	4-4-0	42	"Hesperis"; Leased to D&RGW Ry 5/29/88, returned 8/20/88; Dism 6/30/08.
101	#672-3/73	0-4-4-0T		"Mountaineer"; also called "Modoc" and "Fairlie"; a Vulcan Fairlie type, 4 cyls. 10x18″, 39″ drivers, 62,000 lbs., 9,280 lbs. t.e.; Constructed by Vulcan Foundry Co., Lincolnshire, England; a gift to the D&RG by the Duke of Sutherland, admirer and perhaps investor; Shipped 5/10/73, received 6/20/73, and placed in service in mid-July; Originally numbered 13, Reno. 101 about 1876, and 1001 about 1881; in service intermittently until about 1883; Offered for sale 10/1/87; Dism Burnham 11/1/88.
101	#5441-1881	4-4-0	42	"Col. Boone", 2nd #101; Dism Alamosa 8/31/98.
102	#5681-1881	0-6-0T	48	Sold to Colorado Fuel & Iron Co. #5, 1/28/93, for $3,517.50.
103	#5685-1881	0-6-0T	48	Leased to Pueblo Smelting & Refining Co., 1/2/85 and 3/8/85; Sold to Arkansas Valley Smelter, American Smelting & Refining Co., 2/29/96 for $2,000.
104	#5727-1881	0-6-0T	48	Retired 6/03.
105	#5737-1881	0-6-0T	48	Sold to Rio Grande Southern RR #14, 8/27/91, for $1,200; Sold to Yellow Pine Lumber Co. #4, Mobile, Ala., for $2,200.

106	#5735-1881	0-6-0T	48	Retired 6/03.
107	#6631-1883	4-4-0	42½	Dism Burnham 8/31/98.
108	#6632-1883	4-4-0	42½	To D&RGW Ry #108 7/12/86.
109	#6633-1883	4-4-0	42½	To D&RGW Ry #109 7/12/86.
110-118				See Rio Grande Western (Utah & Pleasant Valley) following.

DENVER & RIO GRANDE RAILWAY,
ATCHISON, TOPEKA & SANTA FE RAILROAD CO., LESSOR

As a result of the 1878 "Royal Gorge War" and costly competition with the Santa Fe, the D&RG was operated under lease for a period in 1878-79 by the Santa Fe road. The lease was negotiated on October 19, 1878, but the Rio Grande was not physically turned over to the Santa Fe's management until December 14. D&RG management, displeased with the arrangement, went to court and as a result the Santa Fe was "dispossessed" of the Rio Grande on June 11, 1879. The D&RG was returned to the AT&SF by Federal court action on July 16, but the lease was finally dissolved by the same court on August 14, 1879, when the D&RG property was placed in the hands of a receiver. During the spring of 1879, the AT&SF purchased five new narrow gauge locomotives for the D&RG, which were removed when the lease was finally set aside. They were as follows:

D&RG No.	
1	Hinkley 1879 — 4-4-0, 12x18″ cyls., 42″ dr., weight approx. 28 tons, cost $5,234.10 — Built as Profile & Franconia Notch (1st)#1 "Echo," diverted and sold to AT&SF; became AT&SF #100 and converted to standard gauge ca. 1880; renamed "Little Buttercup"; probably scrapped by 1898.
301-304	Baldwin #4618, 4621-23, 4/79 — 2-8-0, 15x18″ cyls., 36″ dr., weight approx. 30 tons, total cost $27,200.00 (equivalent to D&RG Class 56) — Became AT&SF #107-110. Leased to Denver, South Park & Pacific RR 7/79 to 1/80, and later used on Silver City, Deming & Pacific RR; converted to standard gauge and scrapped ca. 1892.

CLASS 45

2-6-0 Baldwin 14x20″ 45″ 52,000# 9,560# TE

150	#5643-1881	"Silverton"; Rebuilt 1/15/85; Sold 2/1892 for $2,500 to Bradford, Bordell & Kinzua RR 10, then Buffalo Bradford & Kane 10 in 1904, Big Level & Kinzua 10 in 1905, Baltimore & Ohio in 1911; to West Virginia Midland 9.
151	#5646-1881	"Ruxton"; Leased to B & C Smelting Co. 10/2/83 to 10/12/83; Dism Grand Junction 4/19/02.
152	#5675-1881	"Durango"; Dism Burnham 10/1/99, boiler to Chama.
153	#5784-1881	"Col. Greenwood"; Sold to New Mexico Lumber Co. 1, 7/1895, for $2,250; Reno. Rio Grande & Pagosa Springs 1 ca. 1897, then NML Co. 1 on Rio Grande & Southwestern ca. 1903; Dism.
154	#5785-1881	"Gov. Bent"; Dism Burnham 8/31/98.

CLASS 45½

4-6-0 Baldwin 14x20″ 45″ 53,400# 10,503# TE

158	#5954-1882	To D&RGW Ry 7/12/86, then RGW #20; Sold to Rio Grande Southern RR 22 on 4/1/92; Dism 1916.
159	#5960-1882	To D&RGW Ry 7/12/86, then RGW #21; Sold to Rio Grande Southern RR 23 on 4/1/92; Dism 1916.

(Continued on Page 18)

No. 12, the Las Animas, *was the last of the class 35 light 2-6-0's. (Denver Public Library Western Collection)*

Baldwin Locomotive Works No. 3899, the Delaware *was built for the 1876 Philadelphia Exposition and later became Denver & Rio Grande No. 19, the* Sangre de Cristo. *(The Smithsonian Institution)*

Class 56 2-8-0 No. 52 is shown as the Chama, New Mexico yard engine in early 1908. It had formerly carried the name Music Pass *and would be cut up for scrap that June. (Fred Jukes photo, Richard H. Kindig Collection)*

4-4-0 No. 95, formerly the Embuda, *poses with several admirers at Del Norte, Colorado, in the 1890's. (Richard H. Kindig Collection)*

(Top) Class 42½ No. 108 was the next to the last 4-4-0 purchased by the D&RG (H.L. Broadbelt Collection). (Above) Class 45 2-6-0 No. 152, originally named Durango, has been fitted with footboards and a back-up headlight for switching service (Museum Collection). (Below) Engineer John Kneable, with a large gold watch chain drooping from his belt and his fireman standing at the gangway, proudly stands at the pilot of his locomotive, class 45½ 4-6-0 No. 163, on the Canon City turntable about 1890. Observe the size of the capped stack and oil headlight. (Rio Grande Collection–State Historical Society of Colorado)

Undoubtedly the most unusual locomotive ever to appear on the Rio Grande's roster was the Mountaineer, No. 101, an 0-4-4-0 narrow gauge Fairlie double-ender. It is shown in helper service on La Veta Pass. (Richard H. Kindig Collection)

160	#5963-1882	Dism 6/30/16.
161	#5966-1882	Dism 6/30/16.
162	#5969-1882	Dism 1/5/16.
163	#5970-1882	Rented to Union Pacific Co. 11/9/85 to 1/6/86; Dism. 6/30/16.
164	#5974-1882	Rented to U.P. Co. 11/9/85 to 1/6/86; Dism. 1/8/16.
165	#5977-1882	To D&RGW Ry 7/12/86, then RGW #22; Sold to Rio Grande Southern RR 24 on 4/1/92; Sold 9/1900 to S.S. & W.M. Rice, Hyatt, Texas.

CLASS T-12

4-6-0 Baldwin 14x20" 45" 56,550# 11,590# TE

166	#6664-1883	Dism 11/34.
167	#6671-1883	Dism 11/34.
168	#6670-1883	Donated to Colorado Springs, 7/38.
169	#7028-1883	Donated to Alamosa, Colo., 4/12/41.
170	#7026-1883	Dism 3/26.
171	#7029-1883	Dism 10/26.
172	#7220-1884	Dism 9/36.
173	#7221-1884	Dism 3/26.
174	#7224-1884	Dism 1/37.
175	#7301-1884	Dism 1/37.
176	#7302-1884	Dism 3/26.
177	#7306-1884	Dism 3/26.

Nos. 167, 168 delivered with diamond stack and short smokebox (as Cl. 45½); Nos. 166, 169-177 delivered with straight stack and extended smokebox.

CLASS C-16

2-8-0 Grant 15x20" 36" 60,000# 16,540# TE

200	#1362-1881	"Lake Fork"; Ret 10/26 Dism 12/26.
201	#1363-1881	"Ohio Creek"; Dism 2/37.
202	#1364-1881	"Elk Creek"; Dism 3/26.
203	#1365-1881	"Navajo"; Loaned to Silverton RR; Sold 2/26 to New Mexico Lbr. Co. #4; to Montezuma Lbr. Co.; Dism 1940.
204	#1366-1881	"Crested Buttes"; Dism 10/26.
205	#1367-1881	"Animas Forks"; Ret 10/28, Dism 12/28.
206	#1368-1881	"Hillerton"; Dism 5/36.
207	#1369-1881	"Mt. Holy Cross"; leased to Rio Grande Southern RR at Durango; Dism 10/26.
208	#1370-1881	"Tennessee Pass"; Dism 3/26.
209	#1371-1881	"Home Stake"; Dism 2/37.
210	#1372-1881	"Silver Heel"; Dism 12/34.
211	#1373-1881	"Kirber Creek"; Dism 3/26.
212	#1374-1881	"Antelope"; Dism 12/26.
213	#1375-1881	"Galena Mountain"; Dism 3/26.
214	#1376-1881	"West Cliff"; Dism 6/36.
215	#1377-1881	"Mt. Shavano"; Dism 11/26.
216	#1378-1881	"Red Cliff"; Dism 11/26.
217	#1379-1881	"Grape Creek"; Dism 3/26.
218	#1380-1881	"Antonito"; Dism 12/34.
219	#1381-1881	"Nevada"; Dism 1/35.

220	#1434-1881	Dism 1/35.
221	#1435-1881	Dism 10/26.
222	#1433-1882	Dism 3/26.
223	#1436-1881	Leased to Salt Lake City for display 12/41; to Utah Historical Society 1979.
224	#1437-1882	Dism 10/25/29.
225	#1438-1882	Dism 9/36.
226	#1439-1882	Dism 9/36.
227	#1440-1882	Sold 2/26 to New Mexico Lbr. Co. #5, then Montezuma Lbr. Co.; Dism 1940.

CLASS 60 (C-16) Baldwin

228		Originally D&RG 22; see that number.
229		Originally D&RG 41; see that number.

CLASS C-16 Baldwin

240	#5655-1881	"Lake City"; Dism 3/26.
241	#5654-1881	"Mersereau"; Dism 3/26.
242	#5672-1881	"Barranca"; Sold to Rio Grande Southern 1, 7/28/90; Ret 1903 and Dism 1904.
243	#5670-1881	"Coxo"; Sold to Rio Grande Southern 3, 3/7/91; Ret in 1920s; Dism 1942.
244	#5693-1881	"Rico"; Sold to Rio Grande Southern 4, 12/20/90; Wrecked 1901, Dism 1904.
245	#5689-1881	"Frying Pan"; Sold to Rio Grande Southern 5, 5/12/91; Ret 1903, Dism 1904.
246	#5771-1881	"Otterbees"; Sold to Rio Grande Southern 6, 4/16/91; Dism 1929.
247	#5772-1881	"Pawnee"; Leased to Rio Grande Western 11/28/90 to 1/31/91; Sold to Rio Grande Southern 7, 4/17/91; Ret 1903; Dism 1904.
248	#5801-1881	"Comanche"; Sold to Rio Grande Southern 8, 4/19/91; Ret 1903, Dism 1904.
249	#5800-1881	Sold to Rio Grande Southern 9, 4/19/91; Ret 1903, Dism 1904.
250	#5895-1881	Sold to Rio Grande Southern 10, 8/91; Ret in 1920s; Dism 1942.
251	#5896-1881	Leased to Mather & Geist, 4/84 to 5/84; Sold to Rio Grande Southern 12, 8/91; Ret in 1920s; Dism 1916.
252	#5917-1881	Sold to Rio Grande Southern 13, 8/91; Dism 1916.
253	#5919-1881	Leased to Rio Grande Western 7/29/89 to 2/1/90; Sold to Rio Grande Southern 15, 11/91; Ret in 1920s; Dism 1942.
254	#5923-1881	Sold to Rio Grande Southern 16, 11/91; Ret in 1920s; Dism 1942.
255	#5924-1881	Sold to Rio Grande Southern 17, 11/91; Ret in 1920s; Dism 1942.
256	#5945-1882	Leased to Mather & Geist, 10/82 to 9/83; Sold to Rio Grande Southern 2, 8/15/90; Dism 1916.
257	#5951-1882	Sold to D&RGW Ry 257, 7/12/86; Disp unknown.
258	#5957-1882	Sold to Rio Grande Southern 18, 11/91; Dism 1916.
259	#5956-1882	Sold to Rio Grande Southern 19, 11/91; Dism 1916.
260	#5967-1882	Sold to Rio Grande Southern 20, 11/91; Dism 1916.
261	#5968-1882	Sold to Rio Grande Southern 21, 11/91; Dism 1916.
262	#5996-1882	Dism 3/26.
263	#5995-1882	Dism 10/25/29.
264	#5991-1882	Wrecked and Dism 7/1/89.
265	#5998-1882	Dism 1/35.
266	#6000-1882	Dism 3/26.
267	#6001-1882	Dism 5/26.
268	#6002-1882	Ret 5/55; Donated to Gunnison for Display.
269	#6003-1882	Leased to Rio Grande Western 7/29/89 to 2/1/90; Dism 3/26.

270	#6011-1882	Dism 1/35.
271	#6012-1882	Leased to Rio Grande Western 11/18/89 to 12/28/89; Sold to Montezuma Lumber Co. 12/41; Dism 1947.
272	#6013-1882	Dism 10/26.
273	#6014-1882	Dism 5/26.
274	#6024-1882	Dism 10/26.
275	#6032-1882	To D&RGW Ry 275, 7/12/86, then RGW 101 and 11, rebuilt to standard gauge (65,400# wt. and 14,343# TE); To D&RGW 553 and (1924) 290; Dism 8/24. Placed in Class C-14.
276	#6037-1882	Dism 3/26.
277	#6028-1882	To D&RGW Ry 277, 7/12/86; then RGW 102.
278	#6030-1882	Ret 3/53; Donated to Montrose for display; moved to Cimarron 6/74.
279	#6031-1882	To D&RGW Ry 279, 7/12/86; then RGW 103.
280	#6048-1882	Leased to RGW during June 1890; Dism 10/26.
281	#6049-1882	Leased to RGW, 11/20/89 to 1/30/90; Dism 3/26.
282	#6051-1882	Dism 3/26.
283	#6057-1882	Sold 7/22/33 to Nevada County Narrow Gauge RR 8. Sold Pacific Portland Cement Co. #8, 1943; Dism 5/47.

(Note: Inspection of NCNG 8 by Mr. G. M. Best revealed the builder's plate carried #4938; apparently this boiler, from D&RG 42, had been substituted during shopping and the original boiler from #6057 was given to #42 which became Silverton RR #100.)

284	#6070-1882	Leased to Rio Grande Western, 11/90 to 1/91; Dism 6/36.
285	#6071-1882	Sold to New Mexico Lbr. Co. (2nd)#1 9/8/26; Dism 1940.
286	#6073-1882	Dism 3/26.
287	#6077-1882	To D&RGW Ry 287, 7/12/86, then RGW 104; converted to Standard Gauge; Later on Blacksoler-Miller Lumber RR; Brewton Iron Works; Lindsay Lumber & Export Co. by 9/20.
288	#6095-1882	To D&RGW Ry 288, 7/12/86; then RGW 105.
289	#6097-1882	To D&RGW Ry 289, 7/12/86, then RGW 106; Converted to Standard Gauge; Later on Livingston Lumber RR, and Walker Co. Lumber RR.
290	#6110-1882	To D&RGW Ry 290, 7/12/86, then RGW 107; Converted to Standard Gauge; Later on Lester Mill Co. RR.
291	#6109-1882	To D&RGW Ry 291, 7/12/86, then RGW 108; Converted to Standard Gauge; Later on Red Cypress Lumber RR.
292	#6140-1882	Diverted by builder to Baltimore & Delta RR 4, then Baltimore & Lehigh 4; wrecked and Dism 1899. Not placed in service on D&RG.
293	#6134-1882	Diverted by builder to Baltimore & Delta RR 3, then Baltimore & Lehigh 3; Sold to Banner Lumber Co., becoming Kentwood & Eastern Ry. Not placed in service on D&RG.
294	#6145-1882	To D&RGW Ry 294, 7/12/86; Prob. RGW 109.
295	#6146-1882	To D&RGW Ry 295, 7/12/86; Prob. RGW 110, and converted to Standard Gauge; Later on George Cousin's RR, and Natalbany Lumber Co. RR by 10/06.

Note: For Nos. 287, 288, 290 Standard Gauge, see Standard Gauge listing.

Note: Boiler pressures on Class C-16 engines were generally 160#; However, Nos. 266 and 283 carried 145# and 274, 135#.

Nos. 300-304, see Nos. 417-422

Nos. 305-306, see Nos. 555-554

Nos. 315-320, see Nos. 424-429

Nos. 340-349, see Nos. 400-411

The D&RG had nine of these narrow gauge class 48 0-6-0T's which resembled nothing so much as a Rocky Mountain burro on wheels. They were used in yard service. (G.M. Best Collection)

(Right) T-12 4-6-0 No. 169 is seen at Durango, Colorado, in September 1924. Exhibited at the 1939-40 New York World's Fair, it is today preserved at Alamosa. (H.E. High Photo–Richard H. Kindig Collection). (Right center) C-16 2-8-0 223, built by Grant and pictured in the 1930's has also survived, being displayed in Salt Lake City since 1941. (G.M. Best)

(Right bottom) The 228 shows the original appearance of the Cl. 60 engines, on the Calumet Branch in 1899. (Richard H. Kindig Collection) No. 271 was a Baldwin C-16 serving as the Durango switcher in 1939. (Richard H. Kindig)

CLASS 70

2-8-0 Baldwin 16x20″ 37″ 68,000# 17,055# TE *(See Class C-19)*

In 1888-89 five engines of this class were rebuilt to Standard Gauge Class 74, listed here for convenience.

CLASS 74

2-8-0 Baldwin 16x20″ 36″ 68,700# 17,000# TE

These five engines were converted back to Narrow Gauge 1898-1900, and although renumbered into the 400 series they did not receive their original numbers. All Class 70 engines were rebuilt to conform to new Class C-19.

CLASS C-19

2-8-0 Baldwin 16x20″ 37″ 74,260# 18,947# TE 160# BP

400	#5571-1881	"Green River"; Reno 340; Sold to Knott's Berry Farm 3/12/52, #40.
401	#5572-1881	"Grand River"; To #803, 3/28/89; To 2nd #405, 6/1900; Reno 345; Wrecked 7/17/51 and Dism 9/15/51.
402	#5603-1881	"Shoshone"; To #800, 7/12/88; To 2nd #401, 7/98; Reno 341; Dism 1/39.
403	#5604-1881	"New Mexico"; Reno 343; Dism 4/21/41.
404	#5630-1881	"Sevier"; Reno 344; Dism 1939.
405	#5633-1881	"Utah"; To #804. 4/8/89; To 2nd #410, 9/1900; Reno 349; Sold to New Mexico Lbr. Co., 12/26; Dism 1940.
406	#5712-1881	"Cumbres"; Reno 346; Sold to Montezuma Lumber Co., 5/19/47; Sold to R. W. Richardson, 7/50, then Colorado Railroad Museum.
407	#5713-1881	"Old Rube"; Reno 347; Dism 10/38.
408	#5730-1881	"Marshall Pass"; Reno 348; Dism 1936.
409	#5731-1881	"Red Buttes"; Sold to Rio Grande Southern 41, 11/16; Sold to Knott's Berry Farm #41, 1952.
410	#5755-1881	"Treasury Mountain"; To #801, 6/9/88; To 2nd #411, 12/00; Reno 342; Dism 10/38.
411	#5756-1881	"Quartz Creek"; To #802, 12/88; To 2nd #402, 7/98; Sold to Rio Grande Southern 40, 11/16; Dism 1943.

Renumbering Cross-Reference, 1924 Numbers to Original Numbers:

340 = 400	343 = 403	347 = 407
341 = 402	344 = 404	348 = 408
342 = 410	345 = 401	349 = 405
	346 = 406	

Note: In 1935, Nos. 343, 345 and 346 were leased to the Colorado & Southern Ry. for use on their South Park line between Denver and Leadville. During this use, in 1936, the 346 was wrecked in a runaway on Kenosha Pass, and was rebuilt at Denver's Burlington Shops. All three locomotives were returned to the D&RGW in the spring of 1937, prior to the abandonment of the South Park line.

CLASS C-17

2-8-0 Baldwin 16x20″ 36¾″ 70,300# 17,100# TE 145# BP

417	#8563-1887	Reno 300; Dism 5/36.
418	#8564-1887	Reno 303; Dism 9/35.
419	#8625-1887	Reno 304; Dism 11/34.
420	#8626-1887	Sold to Rio Grande Southern 42, 11/16; Sold to Narrow Gauge Motel, 1953; Sold to Magic Mountain, Denver, 2/58, then Heritage Square.
421	#8629-1887	Reno 301; Dism 5/36.
422	#8632-1887	Reno 302; Dism 10/38.

CLASS C-17

2-8-0 Baldwin 16x20″ 37″ 71,100# 17,100# TE 145# BP

554 1884? Previously Rio Grande Western 1; Reno 306; Dism 1/35.

555 1890? Previously Rio Grande Western 13; Reno 305; Dism 12/27.

Note: These two locomotives were received from the Rio Grande Western Ry., and were not of the same group or design as the earlier D&RG Class C-17. Both were obtained by the RGW upon acquisition of the Utah Central narrow gauge; it is believed that #554 had been Utah Central #1, Baldwin 14487-10/95 (the "1884" notation in D&RG records is believed erroneous), and #555 had been Utah Central #3, originally Great Falls & Canada (Alberta Ry. & Coal Co.) #3, Baldwin 11022-6/90. Upon standard gauging of the UC line, the RGW converted the two to standard gauge, and they were converted back to narrow gauge by the D&RG in 1918.

CLASS C-18

2-8-0 Baldwin 16x20″ 38″ 72,000# 18,325# TE 160# BP

424 #14768-1896 Orig Florence & Cripple Creek RR 7, "W. S. Stratton", then Cripple Creek & Colorado Springs 35; to D&RG 424, 8/20; Reno 320; Dism 10/38.

425 #14352-1895 Orig F&CC RR 3, "Elkton"; to D&RG 425, 8/17; Reno 315; Donated 2/50 to Durango for display.

426 #15246-1897 Orig F&CC RR 11, "Strong"; to D&RG 426, 8/17; Reno 316; Dism 1946.

427 #14513-1895 Orig F&CC RR 5, "Florence"; to D&RG 427, 8/17; Reno 317; Dism Montrose 11/8/48.

428 #14769-1896 Orig F&CC RR 8, "Goldfield"; to D&RG 428, 8/17; Reno 318; Sold 1/31/54 to C. W. Hauck, then Colorado Railroad Museum.

429 #14770-1896 Orig F&CC RR 9, "Alta Vista"; to D&RG 429, 8/17; Reno 319; Rec'd boiler from 320 (ex-424) 12/37; Wrecked 7/17/51 and Dism 9/15/51.

CLASS C-21

2-8-0 Baldwin 17x20″ 38⅞″ 95,650# 20,686# TE 160# BP

430 #17872-1900 Orig Crystal River RR 101; to D&RG 430, 1916; Reno 360; Dism Salida 8/7/50.

431 #17717-1900 Orig Crystal River RR 102; to D&RG 431, 1916; Reno 361; Dism Pueblo 11/15/51.

CLASS C-25

2-8-0 Baldwin 18x20″ 38″ 117,400# 24,641# TE 170# BP

432 #21757-1903 Orig Crystal River RR 103; to D&RG 432, 1916; Reno 375; Dism Alamosa 6/21/49.

CLASS K-27

2-8-2 Baldwin 17x22″ 40″ 136,650# 27,000# TE 200# BP

Note: All engines in this class were constructed in 1903 as Vauclain Compounds, with 13 & 17x22″ cylinders, but were converted to simple (as above) with "D" slide valves in 1907-1909. All except nos. 450, 451, 457 and 460 were later converted to piston valves. Originally equipped with slope-back tenders, all were soon reequipped with larger rectangular tenders.

450	#21677	Dism 1/39.
451	#21685	Dism 1/39.
452	#21803	Dism 7/30/54.
453	#21824	Dism 7/30/54.
454	#21832	Dism 11/6/53.
455	#21845	Sold to Rio Grande Southern 455, 9/39; Wrecked 11/43 and Rebuilt 1947; Dism 1953.
456	#21854	Dism 2/29/52.
457	#21894	Dism 1/39.
458	#21910	Sold 12/41 to National Rys. of Mexico 400, then converted to standard gauge 7/49 and numbered 2250; condemned 1962 and Dism 1963.
459	#21936	Sold 12/41 to National Rys. of Mexico 401, then converted to standard gauge 6/49 and numbered 2251; Dism 3/57.
460	#21728	Dism 1/39.
461	#21729	Sold to Rio Grande Southern 461, 9/30/50; Dism 1953.
462	#21781	Dism 5/16/50.
463	#21788	Sold to Gene Autrey, 5/55; given to town of Antonito, 3/72.
464	#21796	Retired 1962; Sold to Knott's Berry Farm #464, 11/73; sold to Huckleberry RR, Flint, Michigan 1/81.

CLASS K-28

2-8-2 Schenectady 18x22" 44" 156,000# 27,540# TE 200# BP

470-479 #64981-90 1923

Note: Nos. 473, 476 and 478 sold to Durango & Silverton Narrow Gauge Railroad March 1981 and are still in service. Nos. 470-2, 474-5, 477 and 479 were requisitioned by the U.S. Army in October 1942 for use on the White Pass & Yukon as #250-256. After this use, all except #472 were returned to Auburn, Wash., General Army Depot and stored until offered for sale by the war Assets Administration on December 7, 1945; they were purchased by M. Bloch & Co., Seattle, which scrapped them early in 1946. #472 was damaged and shipped from Skagway on March 24, 1944 to Seattle and Northern Pacific Shops at Tacoma, then reshipped to Ogden, Utah, Supply Depot. Also offered on WAA sale of December 7, 1945, and scrapped at Ogden in June 1946, the boiler going to Pueblo Ord. Depot.

CLASS K-36

2-8-2 Baldwin 1925 20x24" 44" 187,100# 36,200# TE 195# BP

480	#58558	Ret 1970; Sold to D&SNG RR 3/81.
481	#58559	Sold to D&SNG RR 3/81.
482	#58541	Ret 1962; To Cumbres & Toltec Scenic RR 1970.
483	#58584	To Cumbres & Toltec Scenic RR 1970.
484	#58585	To Cumbres & Toltec Scenic RR 1970.
485	#58586	Dism 1/24/55.
486	#58587	Ret 1962; To Royal Gorge for display, 12/67.
487	#58588	To Cumbres & Toltec Scenic RR 1970.
488	#58589	To Cumbres & Toltec Scenic RR 1970.
489	#58590	Ret 1962; To Cumbres & Toltec Scenic RR 1970.

In their last years ex-Crystal River outside frame C-25 375 worked the Silverton Branch from Durango (left, Cornelius W. Hauck) and C-21's 360 and 361 served the Gunnison-Montrose route via the Black Canon. (below, Richard H. Kindig) Both classes were known as "little mudhens."

The original and "modern" appearance of the larger narrow gauge 2-8-0's can be compared here. The late Fred Jukes captured the 417 and 404, the latter still with link and pin coupler, awaiting helper turns at Chama, New Mexico and Sargent, Colorado, respectively, during the first decade of the Twentieth Century. Dick Kindig found the 318, all steamed up and ready to go, at Montrose in the summer of 1939.

The most familiar classes of narrow gauge power in later years are pictured here: K-27 No. 454 at Montrose in 1951 (Ross Grenard); K-28 No. 475 at Chama in 1939 (Richard H. Kindig); K-36 No. 481 and K-37 No. 494 at Antonito in 1959 (Gordon W. Roth, William S. Young). All were outside frame 2-8-2's.

Davenport No. 50 replaced steam switchers at Durango in the 1960's. It is pictured below being loaded for its trip to the Roaring Camp & Big Trees Railroad. (A.M. Payne)

CLASS K-37

2-8-2 D&RGW-Baldwin 20x24″ 44″ 187,250# 37,100# TE 200# BP

490 #20695 Ex-#1014, rblt 1928; Ret 1962; Dism 1963-64.

491 #20829 Ex-#1026, rblt 1928; Ret 1970, stored Alamosa.

492 #20749 Ex-#1021, rblt 1928; To Cumbres & Toltec Scenic RR 1970.

493 #20550 Ex.-#1005, rblt 1928; Ret. 1970; Sold to the D&SNG RR 3/81.

494 #20748 Ex-#1020, rblt 1928; Ret 1962; To Cumbres & Toltec Scenic RR 1970.

495 #20522 Ex-#1004, rblt 1928; Ret 1962; To Cumbres & Toltec Scenic RR 1970.

496 #20751 Ex-#1023, rblt 1930; Dism 1/31/55.

497 #20521 Ex-#1003, rblt 1930; Sold to the D&SNG RR 3/81

498 #20640 Ex-#1009, rblt 1930; Sold to the D&SNG RR 3/81.

499 #20753 Ex-#1025, rblt 1930; Ret 1970; Sold to the D&SNG RR 3/81, stored at Alamosa.

Class K-37 engines were rebuilt at Burnham Shops from Class C-41 standard gauge 2-8-0 engines, Baldwin 1902. In March 1981, Nos. 473, 476, 478, 480, 481, 493, 497, 498 and 499 were sold to the Durango & Silverton Narrow Gauge Railroad. No. 499 is stored at Alamosa. No. 491 is being held at Alamosa for the Colorado State Historical Society. Of the locomotives transferred to the Cumbres & Toltec Scenic Railroad, only Nos. 483, 484, 487 and 488 have been in service to date.

DIESEL MECHANICAL

Class DM B
0-4-0 B Davenport-Besler 30″ 60,000# 20,550#TE

50 #2245-5/37 200 hp Caterpillar D-1700 engine. Purchased 12/63 from Edward Hines Lumber Co.; unit was originally Sumpter Valley RR #101. Sold 2/4/70 to Roaring Camp & Big Trees RR. Sold to Durango Railroad Museum 4/81.

Rio Grande Southern Railroad

When Otto Mears built his famed Rio Grande Southern Railroad in 1890-1891, he turned, not surprisingly, to the Rio Grande system for used locomotives to fill his motive power needs. The Rio Grande Western, which had just converted to standard gauge, provided nine 2-8-0s of the small Class 56 type, and four ten-wheelers (three Baldwins and a lone Rome). Similarly the Denver & Rio Grande felt it could spare some narrow gauge power, and provided the backbone of the RGS roster in the form of twenty-two 2-8-0s — nineteen Class C-16, one Class C-17, and two of the "big" Class C-19s. In addition, the D&RG supplied one ancient mogul, one eightwheeler and an 0-6-0T. The latter three and most of the Class 56 2-8-0s were disposed of by the turn of the century, and better D&RG locomotives leased or rented when traffic demanded — which then was not often.

The next change of importance in the roster occurred in 1916, when the RGS replaced the remaining three original tenwheelers with three big "new" 1899-1900 Schenectadys obtained from the defunct Florence & Cripple Creek. The largest engines on the RGS at the time, they weighed 85,000 pounds and boasted 18,651 pounds tractive effort; cylinders were 16x20″, drivers 42″ dia., and boiler pressure 180 pounds. Of this group, famous "movie star" No. 20 is preserved by the Rocky Mountain Railroad Club at the Colorado Railroad Museum.

The C-16s were also gradually retired, many rusting away in a deadline at Durango for years. During the thirties "mudhen" 2-8-2s (Class K-27) were leased from the D&RGW as needed for the less-than-frequent freights, with No. 455 being acquired through trade in 1939, and ownership of No. 461 being effected in 1950. Finally, former Colorado & Southern No. 74 was purchased from Morse Brothers, Denver scrap dealers, in 1948. This Brooks 2-8-0 had been built in 1898 for the Colorado & Northwestern (their No. 30), and weighed in at 95,500 pounds, with 16x20″ cylinders and 37″ drivers.

The roster below traces the origins and dispositions of the various locomotives. With the exception of the Schenectady and Brooks locomotives discussed above, mechanical specifications of the engines will be found under the appropriate D&RG and RGW entries.

NO.	TYPE	BUILDER	NO./DATE	NOTES:
1	2-8-0	Baldwin	5672-1881	Orig. D&RG 242, "Barranca," to RGS July 28, 1890. Scrapped 1904.
1	2-8-0	Baldwin	5200-1880	Ex-BC&F 1; See No. 35.
2	2-8-0	Baldwin	5945-1882	Orig. D&RG 256, to RGS Aug. 15, 1890. Scrapped 1916.
3	2-8-0	Baldwin	5670-1881	Orig. D&RG 243, "Coxo," to RGS March 7, 1891. Retired 1920s. Dismantled 1942.
4	2-8-0	Baldwin	5693-1881	Orig. D&RG 244, "Rico," to RGS Dec. 13, 1890. Wrecked 1901. Dismantled 6/1903.
5	2-8-0	Baldwin	5689-1881	Orig. D&RG 245, "Frying Pan," to RGS May 12, 1891. Dismantled 1904.
6	2-8-0	Baldwin	5771-1881	Orig. D&RG 246, "Otterbees," to RGS April 16, 1891. To D&RGW 9/24/38. Sold for scrap 10/1/38.
7	2-8-0	Baldwin	5772-1881	Orig. D&RG 247, "Pawnee," to RGS April 19, 1891. Dismantled 1904.
8	2-8-0	Baldwin	5801-1881	Orig. D&RG 248, "Comanche," to RGS April 19, 1891. Dismantled 1904.
9	2-8-0	Baldwin	5800-1881	Orig. D&RG 249, to RGS April 16, 1891. Dismantled 1904.
10	2-8-0	Baldwin	5895-1881	Orig. D&RG 250, to RGS April 9, 1891. Retired 1920s. Dismantled 1942.
11	2-6-0	Baldwin	4336-1878	Orig. D&RG 29, "Cochetope," to A. T. Sullenberger #1 in 1888. traded back to D&RG 11/8/1888, sold to RGS Jan. 2, 1891. Sold to George M. Dilley & Son 1899.
12	2-8-0	Baldwin	5896-1881	Orig. D&RG 251, to RGS Aug. 1, 1891. Retired 1920s. Dismantled 1942.
13	2-8-0	Baldwin	5917-1881	Orig. D&RG 252, to RGS Aug. 1, 1891. Dismantled 1916.
14	0-6-0T	Baldwin	5737-1881	Orig. D&RG 105, to RGS Aug. 14, 1891. Sold to Yellow Pine Lumber Co., Mobile, Ala., 11/1899.
15	2-8-0	Baldwin	5919-1881	Orig. D&RG 253, to RGS Dec. 11, 1891. Retired 1920s. Dismantled 1942.
16	2-8-0	Baldwin	5923-1881	Orig. D&RG 254, to RGS Dec. 23, 1891. Retired 1920s. Dismantled 1942.
17	2-8-0	Baldwin	5924-1881	Orig. D&RG 255, to RGS Nov. 1891. Retired 1920s. Dismantled 1942.
18	2-8-0	Baldwin	5957-1882	Orig. D&RG 258, to RGS Oct. 26, 1891. Dismantled 1916.
19	2-8-0	Baldwin	5956-1882	Orig. D&RG 259, to RGS Dec. 22, 1891. Dismantled 1916.
20	2-8-0	Baldwin	5967-1882	Orig. D&RG 260, to RGS Oct. 2, 1891. Dismantled 1916.
20	4-6-0	Schenectady	5007-1899	Orig. F&CC 20, "Portland," to RGS 1/1916. Sold 1952 to Rocky Mountain Railroad Club; Display, Colorado Railroad Museum, Golden, Colo.
21	2-8-0	Baldwin	5968-1882	Orig. D&RG 261, to RGS Nov. 1891. Dismantled 1916.
22	4-6-0	Baldwin	5954-1882	Orig. D&RG 158, to D&RGW 7/12/86, RGW 20, to RGS 22 4/11/1892. Dismantled 1916.
22	4-6-0	Schenectady	5421-1900	Orig. F&CC 24, "Last Dollar," to RGS 1/1916. Out of service 1942. Dismantled 1946.
23	4-6-0	Baldwin	5960-1882	Orig. D&RG 159, to D&RGW 7/12/86, RGW 21, to RGS 4/11/1892. Dismantled 1916.
24	4-6-0	Baldwin	5977-1882	Orig. D&RG 165, to D&RGW 7/12/86, RGW 22, to RGS 4/1/1892. Sold to S. S. & W. M. Rice, Hyatt, Tex., 9/1900.
25	4-6-0	New York Loco. Works	90-1884 (Rome)	Orig. Denver Circle 7, to RGW 31, to RGS 1891. Dismantled 1916.
25	4-6-0	Schenectady	5008-1899	Orig. F&CC 21, "Isabella," to RGS 1/1916. Dismantled 1940. Tender to 2nd 20.
27	2-8-0	Baldwin	5136-1880	Orig. D&RG 71, "Pacific Slope," to D&RGW 71, 7/12/86, RGW 71, to RGS 27, 1891; to Carolina & Northwestern 230, 9/27/99, to Gainesville Midland, to Southern Iron & Equipment Co. #969, to Compania Azucarera de Altamaria 3, Havana, Cuba 10/8/1915.

NO.	TYPE	BUILDER	NO./DATE	NOTES:
28	2-8-0	Baldwin	5137-1880	Orig. D&RG 72, "Piedra," to D&RGW 72, 7/12/86, RGW 72, to RGS 28, 1891. Sold to Morenci Southern 1, 1900 (Detroit Copper Mining Co.).
29	2-8-0	Baldwin	5138-1880	Orig. D&RG 73, "Sneffels," to D&RGW 73, 7/12/86, RGW 73, to RGS 29, 1891. Sold to Morenci Southern 2, 1900 (Detroit Copper Mining Co.).
30	2-8-0	Baldwin	5164-1880	Orig. D&RG 74, "Hermano," to D&RGW 74, 7/12/86, RGW 74, to RGS 1891, to RGW 1899, 04, to Sumpter Valley 7 in 1900, Re-No. 10. Scrapped 1936.
31	2-8-0	Baldwin	5184-1880	Orig. D&RG 76, "U. S. Mountain," to D&RGW 76, 7/12/86, RGW 76, to RGS 1891, to Morenci Southern 3, 1900 (Detroit Copper Mining Co.), to Franklin & Abbeville, to Nacozari RR.
32	2-8-0	Baldwin	5185-1880	Orig. D&RG 77, "Rinconida," to D&RGW 77, 7/12/86, to RGW 77, to RGS 32, 1891. To SG&N 32, 1899. Dismantled c. 1910, boiler at Teffts Spur Sawmill site, below Silverton.
33	2-8-0	Baldwin	5225-1880	Orig. D&RG 78, "Sandia," to D&RGW 78, 7/12/86, to RGS 33, 1891. To George M. Dilley & Son, 1899. Returned 1901, to SG&N 33, 1902. Dismantled c. 1903.
34	2-8-0	Baldwin	5226-1880	Orig. D&RG 79, "La Plata," to D&RGW 79, 7/12/86, RGW 79, to RGS, 1891, to Silverton RR 101, 1892, then S.N. 1 in 1896. Dismantled 1920s.
34	Shay	Lima	269-1890	Purchased by Otto Mears for use on Silverton RR. Used by RGS during construction out of Durango. Traded 34 (2-8-0) for Shay in 1892. Used on Black Hawk-Enterprise Branch. Sold Siskiwit & Iron River Ry. 7/7/99 (Ashland Lbr. Co.), Ashland, Wisc., to Thompson Bros. Lbr. Co., Doucette, Tex., to Fidelity Lbr. Co., Doucette, Tex., Turkey Creek Lbr. Co., Waynesboro, Miss., Stark & Oldham Bros. Lbr. Co., Waynesboro, Miss.
35	2-8-0	Baldwin	5200-1880	Orig. D&RG 80, "Chico," to D&RGW 80, 7/12/86, RGW 80, RGS 35 1891, stored at Burnham Shops, to Boston Coal & Fuel Co. 1, (Calumet Fuel Co. 1), RGS 2nd 1. Dismantled 1913.
36	4-4-0	Baldwin	5119-1880	Orig. D&RG 93, "Roaring Fork," to RGS Dec. 2, 1891. Sold Arkansas Lbr. Co., Lester, Ark.
40	2-8-0	Baldwin	5756-1881	Orig. D&RG 411, "Quartz Creek," Re-No. 802 12/88, to 2nd 402 7/1898, to RGS 11/1916. Dismantled 1943.
41	2-8-0	Baldwin	5731-1881	Orig. D&RG 409, "Red Buttes," to RGS 41 11/1916, to Knott's Berry Farm, Buena Park, Calif. 11/1951.
42	2-8-0	Baldwin	8626-1887	Orig. D&RG 420, to RGS 11/1916, to Narrow Gauge Motel, Alamosa 1953, to Magic Mountain, Denver Amusement Park, 2/1958, to Woodmoor Corp., Monument, Colo. (Display) 2/6/69. To Heritage RR Co., Golden, Colo. 5/9/71. On display.
74	2-8-0	Brooks	2951-1898	Orig. Colorado & Northwestern 30, Denver, Boulder & Western 30, to Morse Bros. Machinery & Supply Co., Denver, 1919. To Colorado & Southern 74, 1921. To Morse Bros. 1945, to RGS 74 11/1948. Sold to City of Boulder, Colo., 1952. On Display.
455	2-8-2	Baldwin	21832-1903	Orig. D&RGW 455; Traded to RGS 9/1939 for RGS Ditcher 030. Wrecked 11/1943, rebuilt 1947. Scrapped 1953.
461	2-8-2	Baldwin	21729-1903	Orig. D&RGW 461; to RGS 9/30/1950. Dismantled 1953.

MOTORS (GALLOPING GEESE)

1	Buick	6/31	Scrapped 1933.
2	Buick-Pierce	8/31	To Colorado Railroad Museum.
3	Pierce-GMC-Wayne	12/31	To Knott's Berry Farm.
4	Pierce-GMC-Wayne	5/32	To Telluride.
5	Pierce-GMC-Wayne	6/33	To Dolores.
6	Buick-Pierce	1/34	To Brinkerhoff; to Durango Railroad Museum 1982.
7	Ford-Pierce	10/36	To Brinkerhoff; to Durango Railroad Museum 1982.

Rio Grande Southern

Rio Grande Southern goose No. 4 is shown in front of the Ridgway depot in August 1940. After World War II, Nos. 3-5 were rebuilt with Wayne bus bodies. (Grahame Hardy Collection)

2-8-0 No. 9 poses (below) on Lizard Head Pass about 1895, westbound with the business car Rico. (William Henry Jackson Photo—Colorado State Historical Society)

Latter day power on the Southern is represented by the 461 at Trout Lake and the 25 near Durango (below, left and right, Museum collection) and ex-DB&W, ex-C&S 2-8-0 No. 74 helping borrowed D&RGW mudhen 452 with a stock extra near Placerville in September 1951. (bottom, Robert W. Richardson photo)

Rio Grande Western Railway

The table below lists all of the narrow gauge locomotives known to have been received or acquired by the Denver & Rio Grande Western Ry. (Utah) prior to 1889. The first nine were small, ancient (1873-1879) locomotives acquired through the absorption of three Utah shortlines — the Utah & Pleasant Valley, the Wasatch & Jordan Valley, and the Bingham Canon & Camp Floyd. Details of these locomotives are set forth under U&PV below. As a part of the terms of termination of the D&RG lease of the D&RGW Ry. in 1886, 27 D&RG locomotives were transferred to the D&RGW Ry. Finally, the D&RGW Ry. purchased two used Rome tenwheelers from the Denver Circle Railroad. These locomotives were renumbered into a new numbering sequence as shown in the 1890 Rio Grande Western roster. The precise date of this renumbering is not known; at least some of the locomotives — the "U&PV" and ex-Denver Circle engines — carried their new numbers as early as 1887. Subsequently, with the acquisition of the Utah Central RR in 1898, a number of narrow gauge engines were received, of which three Baldwin 2-8-0s (one only 3 years old) were retained for operation of the line (with the assistance of an ex-RGW 2-8-0 hastily repurchased from the RGS, who had bought it in 1891, and a "widened-out" RGW 2-8-0 temporarily converted back to narrow gauge) until the UC was relaid to standard gauge.

Narrow Gauge Locomotives

CLASS			OLD NOS.			RGW NUMBERS				
1890	1895	1902	D&RG	D&RGW	UC	1890	1892	1899	1900	NOTES:
—	—	—	112	3	—	1	—	—	—	Out by 9/90
—	—	—	110	1	—	2	—	—	—	Out by 9/90; Sold to Fitzhugh Luther & Co. 7/19/03.
—	—	—	111	2	—	3	—	—	—	Out by 9/90; Dism 10/3/03 Salt Lake City.
—	—	—	113	4	—	4	—	—	—	Out by 9/90; Sold to Fitzhugh Luther & Co. 7/27/03.
—	—	—	114	5	—	5	—	—	—	Out by 9/90; Sold to Fitzhugh Luther & Co. 7/27/03.
35	—	—	115	6	—	6	6	—	—	Rblt to 2-6-0; out during 1892; Sold to Fitzhugh Luther & Co. 9/29/03.
—	—	—	116	7	—	7	—	—	—	Dism. 3/90, boiler to Scofield for stationary use. Other records show sold to Fitzhugh Luther & Co. 11/9/03.
—	—	—	117	8	—	8	—	—	—	Out by 9/90; Sold to Fitzhugh Luther & Co. 11/9/03.
35	—	—	118	9	—	9	9	—	—	Rblt. to 2-6-0; out during 1892; Sold to Fitzhugh Luther & Co. 7/03.
41½	—	—	108	—	—	15	—	—	—	To Cl. 42½, 1891; destroyed 4/91.
41½	—	—	109	—	—	16	—	—	—	To Cl. 42½, 1891; out by 12/91.
45½	—	—	158	—	—	20	—	—	—	To Rio Grande Southern RR 22, 1891.
45½	—	—	159	—	—	21	—	—	—	To Rio Grande Southern RR 23, 1891.
45½	—	—	165	—	—	22	—	—	—	To Rio Grande Southern RR 24, 1891.
47	14	—	—	—	—	30	1	—	—	Ex-Denver Circle 4 or 5, Rome 87 or 88, 6/84; purchased by 1887; Reblt. SG 1891; out during 1898.
47	—	—	—	—	—	31	—	—	—	Ex-Denver Circle 7, Rome 90, 6/84; To Rio Grande Southern RR 24, 11/91.
56	15	64	81	—	—	70	14	14	14	Rblt. SG 1898; out 1902-03; Sold to Fitzhugh Luther & Co. 7/03.
56	—	—	71	—	—	71	—	—	—	To Rio Grande Southern RR 27, 1891.
56	—	—	72	—	—	72	—	—	—	To Rio Grande Southern RR 28, 1891.
56	—	—	73	—	—	73	—	—	—	To Rio Grande Southern RR 29, 1891.
56	15	—	74	—	—	74	—	04	—	To Rio Grande Southern RR 30, 1891; repurchased from RGS 1899; to Sumpter Valley Ry. 7, 1900, then 10; retired 1924.
56	15	64	75	—	—	75	2	2	—	Rblt. SG 1891; out 1902-03.
56	—	—	76	—	—	76	—	—	—	To Rio Grande Southern RR 31, 1891.
56	—	—	77	—	—	77	—	—	—	To Rio Grande Southern RR 32, 1891.
56	—	—	78	—	—	78	—	—	—	To Rio Grande Southern RR 33, 1891.
56	—	—	79	—	—	79	—	—	—	To Rio Grande Southern RR 34, 1891.
56	—	—	80	—	—	80	—	—	—	To Rio Grande Southern RR 35, 1891.
60	15	65	257	—	—	100	3	3	3	Rblt. SG 1891; out 1902-03.
60	15	65	275	—	—	101	11	11	11	Rblt. SG 1893; to D&RG 553, 1909.
60	15	65	277	—	—	102	12	12	12	Rblt. SG 1898; out 1903; Sold to Fitzhugh Luther & Co. 8/04.
60	15	65	279	—	—	103	5	5	5	Rblt. SG 1891; out 1902-03.

CLASS			OLD NOS.			RGW NUMBERS				
1890	1895	1902	D&RG	D&RGW	UC	1890	1892	1899	1900	NOTES:
60	15	65	287	—	—	104	6	6	6	Rblt. SG 1891; sold 1902-03.
60	15	—	288	—	—	105	13	13	—	Out 1899.
60	15	65	289	—	—	106	7	7	7	Rblt. SG 1890; sold 1903-08.
60	15	65	290	—	—	107	9	9	9	Rblt. SG 1890; sold 1902-03.
60	15	65	291	—	—	108	4	4	4	Rblt. SG 3/90; sold 1902-03.
60	15	65	294	—	—	109	8	8	8	Rblt. SG 1890; rblt. NG 10/99; rblt. SG 1900; out 1903-08.
60	15	65	295	—	—	110	10	10	10	Rblt. SG 3/90; Sold to Fitzhugh Luther & Co. 9/27/03.
—	16	77	—	—	1	—	—	01	01	Ex-Utah Central; reblt SG 1900; to D&RG 554, 1909. Baldwin 14487, 10/95;
—	15	—	—	—	2	—	—	2	—	Ex-Utah Central; out 1900.
—	16	77	—	—	3	—	03	03	13	Ex-Utah Central; orig Alberta Ry. & Coal Co. 3, Baldwin 11022, 6/90; to UC Ry. 1895; rblt. SG 7/1900; to D&RG 555, 1/31/09.

Specifications

Listed at right are mechanical data for the ex-Denver Circle and Utah Central locomotives. Data for all others will be found under the appropriate D&RG listings.

NOS.	TYPE	CYLINDERS	DRIVERS	ENG. WT.
30, 31	4-6-0	14x20″	45″	56,000#
01, 03	2-8-0	16x20″	36″	72,000#
02	2-8-0	15x18″	36″	56,000#

Standard Gauge Locomotives

Standard gauge locomotives of the Rio Grande Western will be found listed under their succeeding D&RG numbers. The following chart provides the renumbering sequences.

RGW	D&RG	RGW	D&RG
21-23	805-807	200-203	940-943
33-42	540-549	300-303	960-963
51-54	503-506	400-403	970-973
61, 62, 66	550-552	500-505	950-955
63-65, 70-73	712-718	600-604	980-984
80-83	740-743	700-704	990-994
111-153	630-672	1180-1199	1180-1199

THE UTAH & PLEASANT VALLEY LOCOMOTIVES.

During 1872-73, two small narrow gauge roads were begun in Utah, both building out from the present town of Sandy. The first, the Bingham Canyon & Camp Floyd (originally, Bingham Canyon & Salt Lake, and frequently simply "Bingham Canyon"), built west from Sandy up to the mining camp of Bingham Canyon. The second, the Wasatch & Jordan Valley, built east from Sandy towards the mining camps of Alta and Cottonwood. Both roads featured steep grades; the W&JV in 1875 boasted 9 miles of new snowshed to permit year-'round operation!

The two roads were begun as separate enterprises. The BC quickly came under the control of a group headed by a New Yorker named C. W. Scofield; and by 1875 Scofield was also President of the W&JV. The two roads were finally officially merged in 1878, as the W&JV.

Meanwhile, the Scofield group became interested in a new undertaking — the Utah & Pleasant Valley. This 3′ gauge road was projected and eventually built from Provo to coal mines at Pleasant Valley to the southeast — near the present town of Scofield. Although indications of activity on this line occur as early as 1876, it is not recorded as completed until October, 1879.

The three little lines were apparently not a resounding financial success, and both the U&PV and W&JV (which still retained its merged corporate individuality to an extent) defaulted on their 7% mortgage bonds in 1881-82. A foreclosure sale was held on June 13, 1882, at which time the parent U&PV (and, subsequently, the W&JV) was purchased by the new Denver & Rio Grande *Western* Railway of Utah. The little roads were no doubt considered valuable by the Palmer forces as feeders and for their charters — and potential nuisances if not bought up. Parts of the U&PV right-of-way were then used in constructing the D&RGW Ry. line from Ogden and Salt Lake City to Grand Junction.

No records are known to exist of the D&RGW Railway's early narrow gauge roster, but D&RG records indicate that prior to April 1883 the D&RGW Ry had nine small locomotives, numbered 1-9, which were then referred to as "Utah & Pleasant Valley" locomotives. It is believed that these nine were received by the D&RGW Ry as a result of the 1882 U&PV purchase; were used in construction and other service until completion of the D&RGW Ry early in 1883; and were subsequently used in light service in Utah for some years thereafter.

Upon completion of the D&RGW Ry, the U&PV engines carried the numbers 1-9 — probably the numbers assigned to them by the U&PV sometime prior to 1882. To avoid confusion with D&RG Nos. 1-9, these locomotives were renumbered in April, 1883, to 110-118. However, in September, 1884, they were deleted from the D&RG roster with the notation "Returned to Utah & Pleasant Valley". More likely, D&RG officials belatedly recognized that they were not D&RG property and merely dropped them from D&RG records. An 1885 list of D&RG locomotives notes the 110-118 as "Utah" and excludes them from the total.

It should also be remembered that a contract signed on August 1, 1882, provided for operation of the Western, upon completion, by the D&RG. However, subsequent financial reverses and receivership of the D&RG, and accompanying changes in management, led to abrogation of the contract and a serious disruption of relations between the two roads, and resulted in independent operation of the Western for over two decades. In settlement of litigation over the contract termination, on July 12, 1886, the D&RG transferred 27 narrow gauge engines to the Western; and these, plus the remainder of the nine "U&PV" engines, formed the basis of the D&RGW Ry narrow gauge roster.

While an entry for D&RG 110-118 appears in official D&RG locomotive rosters, it is not believed to be entirely correct. The following compilation, from both D&RG and other sources, is offered as a tentative record of these locomotives.

U&PV/ D&RGW No.	D&RG No.	Type	Cyl.	Driver Dia.	Rigid Whlbase.	Boiler Dia.	Engine Wt. (lbs.)	
1	110	0-6-0	11x16″	36″	8′9½″	35″	26,000	W&JV #1 "Chamois", Dawson & Baily, rec'd 2/73, orig 2-6-0, six wheel tender.
2	111	0-6-0	11x16″	36″	8′9½″	35″	26,000	W&JV #2 "Deseret", Dawson & Baily, rec'd 9/73, orig 2-6-0 or 2-4/2-0 (see below), six wheel tender.
3	112	0-6-0	12x16″	36″	8′1″	36″	30,800	BC&CF #2 "Winamuck" (?), Porter #188-1/74.
4	113	0-6-0	12x16″	36″	8′1″	36″	30,800	BC&CF #3(?), Porter #189-1/74 or 3/74.
5	114	4-4-0	12x16″	32″	4′0″	36″	30,800	W&JV #3, Dawson & Baily 1874.
6	115	0-6-0	12x16″	36″	8′11″	36″	30,800	BC&CF #4 (?), Porter #207-2/75.
7	116	2-6-0	12x16″	36″	11′8″	37″	40,000	Prob. U&PV #3, Baldwin #4048-1/77, orig Galveston, Brazos & Colorado #3, returned and resold to U&PV 12/79.
8	117	0-6-0	12x16″	32″	8′11″	36″	30,800	Prob. U&PV #2; believed built for Colorado Central RR, Porter #276-8/77, diverted and sold to U&PV.
9	118	0-6-0	12x16″	36″	8′11″	36″	30,800	Prob. U&PV #1, orig BC&CF #1, Porter 1873, transferred to U&PV ca. 1877.

Note: The precise design of W&JV #2 is somewhat of a mystery. It was described at the time as being "intended to work a grade of some 500 feet to the mile" for which purpose the "hind drivers have a grooved tire that is applied to the rail by a small steam cylinder (that) can be applied to give any amount of adhesion needed". This may have been an invention of a Col. James S. French of the Washington & Alexander RR, which involved a "third or supplementary pair of driving wheels . . . swung in the rear of the ordinary drivers, and connected with the latter so as to revolve at the same rate of speed. These additional drivers have a grooved tread, and are hung in such a manner as to be lifted from contact with the track at the will of the engineer". If this marvel was intended to work on the 11% grades of the W&JV's extension from Wasatch up to the mines at Alta, it was a failure, as later accounts state that the grade was "too heavy for the most powerful engines (and) the cars are drawn by horses over this portion of the road". Apparently the oddity was rebuilt into an orthodox 0-6-0.

STANDARD GAUGE LOCOMOTIVES

Note: in researching individual locomotives, it should be kept in mind that the majority of Rio Grande locomotives were renumbered in 1924, as set forth in the chart below. For locomotives in service post-1924, their original numbers should be ascertained from the chart; those not shown retained their original numbers.
The American Locomotive Company was formed in June 1901 by a merger of eight locomotive manufacturers. Subsequently the Rio Grande purchased steam power built by three of the Alco plants—Schenectady, Brooks and Richmond. See Classes K-28, T-29, S-33, C-48, F-81, M-67, M-78, L-62, L-96, L-76, L-107, L-131, L-132 and L-97.

Renumbering Charts

1924 Renumbering

NEW	*OLD*	*NEW*	*OLD*	*NEW*	*OLD*	*NEW*	*OLD*	*NEW*	*OLD*	*NEW*	*OLD*
10	412	520	713	592-595	952-955	622	672	661	601	761	777
20-22	805-807	521	712	596-597	950-951	623	663	662-667	622-627	763	760
50-62	831-843	525	718	600	630	624	664	668	595	777	761
287	680	526-528	715-717	601	631	625	639	669	629	800	1006
288	681	530-533	740-743	602	652	626	662	670	600	801-805	1001-05
500	545	540-544	700-704	603	647	630-634	570-574	671	594	900-903	960-963
501	548	535-539	705-709	604-607	634-637	635	566	672-675	602-605	915	958
505	512	545-546	710-711	608	650	636-642	556-562	676-680	576-580	930-934	990-994
506	524	575	821	609	649	643	569	681	555	940-944	980-984
507	533	576	826	610	640	644-645	564-565	682-687	582-587	950	915
508	528	577	822	611	641	646-647	606-607	688	596	951-964	901-914
511	508	578	806	612	642	648	592	689	589	1000	1130
512	530	579	819	613	646	649-656	609-616	690	599	1001-29	1101-29
513	534	590	940	614-620	654-660	657	593	691	591	1400-09	1250-59
514	529	591	942	621	670	658-660	618-620	760	763		

Rio Grande Western Renumbering

RGW	*D&RG*	*RGW*	*D&RG*	*RGW*	*D&RG*	*RGW*	*D&RG*
51-54	503-506	11	553	80-83	740-743	300-303	960-963
61	550	13	555	21-23	805-807	400-403	970-973
62	551	111-153	630-672	836-840	836-840	600-604	980-984
66	552	63-65	712-714	200-203	940-943	700-704	990-994
1	554	70-73	715-718	500-505	950-955	1180-99	1189-99

CLASS 75

2-8-0 Baldwin 1881 16x20" 36" 69,000# 16,320# TE

412 #5850 Reno 550, 1887.

413 #5845 Reno 551, 1887.

414 #5857 Reno 552, 1887.

415 #5860 Reno 553, 1887.

416 #5928 Reno 554, 1887.

These engines renumbered to 550-554 in 1887, and subsequently rebuilt as 0-8-0T, Class S-19; consult those numbers and class.

CLASS 46

4-6-0 Baldwin 14x20" 45" 55,600# 10,140# TE

155 #5934-1881 Reno 503, 10/87; Sold 4/06 to J. E. Brown; Later on John L. Roper Lumber RR, Kinston Lumber.

156 #5936-1881 Reno 504, 10/87; Sold to Denver, Lakewood & Golden RR 6/99.

157	#5949-1881	Reno 505, 10/87; Sold to J. E. Brown, 4/06.	Some sources indicate these three locomotives were originally named "Uncle Sam", "Trinidad" and "Salida" in that order. After 1887 No. 505 (ex-157) carried the name "Uncle Sam", and when it was scrapped in 1906 the name was given to No. 502 (below).

CLASS 76

4-6-0 Baldwin 16x24″ 56″ 78,300# 12,605# TE

500	#6533-1883	"Denver"; Dism 12/23.
501	#6534-1883	"Manitou"; Dism 1/16.
502	#8636-1887	"Pueblo"; Dism 1/16.

CLASS 104

4-6-0 Rome 17x24″ 60″ 104,200# 15,463# TE

503	#568-1890	From Rio Grande Western 51; Dism 1/1916.
504	#569-1890	From RGW 52; Dism 2/1916.
505	#570-1890	From RGW 53; Dism 12/1915.
506	#571-1890	From RGW 54; Dism 1/1916.

CLASS T-18

4-6-0 Baldwin 18x24″ 55″ 109,000# 19,230# TE 160# BP

Originally built with 54″ drivers, some were rebuilt with 58½″ drivers and 17,925# TE.

506	#8876-1887	"Trinidad"; Reno 512 in 1908; Reno 505; Dism 12/26.
507	#8877-1887	"Salida"; Dism 1924.
508	#8883-1887	"Buena Vista"; Reno 511; Dism 8/24.
509	#9107-1888	"Leadville"; Dism 8/24.
510	#9108-1888	"Glenwood"; Dism 1924.
511	#9111-1888	"Aspen"; Dism 1924.
512	#10503-1889	Sold to Colorado & Wyoming RR 1/29/03.
513	#10499-1889	Dism 2/24.
514	#10518-1889	Dism 3/24.
515	#11146-1890	Dism 3/24.
516	#11147-1890	Dism 2/26.
517	#11156-1890	Dism 8/20.
518	#11153-1890	Dism 3/24.
519	#11186-1890	Dism 8/20.
520	#11191-1890	Dism 1/16.
521	#11189-1890	Dism 8/20.
522	#11192-1890	Dism 8/20.
523	#11193-1890	Dism 8/20.
524	#11187-1890	Reno 506; Dism 8/24.
525	#11197-1890	Dism 3/24.
526	#11199-1890	Dism 3/26.
527	#11201-1890	Dism 3/24.
528	#11635-1891	Reno 508; Dism 12/26.
529	#11636-1891	Reno 514; Dism 8/24.
530	#11727-1891	Reno 512; Dism 8/24.
531	#11761-1891	Dism 3/24.
532	#11717-1891	Sold to Crystal River & San Juan RR #1, 11/15 and Dism 2/1924.
533	#11723-1891	Reno 507; Dism 3/26.
534	#11731-1891	Reno 513; Dism 8/24.
535	#11720-1891	Dism 3/24.
536	#11718-1891	Dism 3/24.
537	#11725-1891	Dism 3/24.
538	#11869-1891	Dism 3/24.

(Above) The first standard gauge locomotives such as No. 414 were identical to the largest narrow gauge 2-8-0's. (Baldwin Magazine, Museum Collection). Rio Grande Western No. 41 at Salt Lake City was a product of the Rome Locomotive Works. (Rio Grande Collection, State Historical Society of Colorado)

Two of the earliest classes of ten wheelers are represented above by No. 501, the Manitou, at Denver Union Depot and No. 157. (Joseph Sturtevant photo, Richard H. Kindig Collection; H.L. Broadbelt Collection) T-18 No. 510 (below) was one of many 4-6-0's and 2-8-0's acquired at the time of standard gauging the main line to Salt Lake City in 1887-1890. (Otto Perry photo, Denver Public Library Western History Collection)

RIO GRANDE
ROYAL GORGE
MOFFAT TUNNEL
SCENIC LINE OF THE WORLD

CLASS T-17

4-6-0 Rome 18x24" 60" 114,800# 17,075# TE 155# BP

540 #536-1889 Orig RGW 33; Dism 2/24.

541 #537-1889 Orig RGW 34; Dism 2/24.

542 #538-1889 Orig RGW 35; Dism 2/24.

543 #539-1889 Orig RGW 36; Sold to Deep Creek Ry. #1, 11/16; Dism 9/30.

544 #540-1890 Orig RGW 37; Dism 2/24.

545 #541-1890 Orig RGW 38; Reno 500; Dism 3/26.

546 #672-1891 Orig RGW 39; Sold to Western Pacific 126, 8/17; Sold to Tidewater Southern 1, 1/18; Ret 11/46, Dism 10/47.

547 #673-1891 Orig RGW 40; Dism 2/16.

548 #674-1891 Orig RGW 41; Reno 501; Dism 3/26.

549 #675-1891 Orig RGW 42; Sold to Western Pacific 127, 8/17; Ret 12/23, Dism 6/30.

CLASS S-19

0-8-0T Baldwin 1881 16x20" 36" 64,900# 16,320# TE

The following locomotives were originally Class 75 2-8-0, rebuilt prior to 1900 as 0-8-0T type and renumbered 800-804 in 1908.

550 #5850 Ex-412, Reno 550; Reno 800, 1908; Reno 10, 1924; Dism 12/27.

551 #5845 Ex-413, Reno 551; Reno 801 and Dism 2/15.

552 #5857 Ex-414, Reno 552; Reno 802 and Dism prior to 1924.

553 #5860 Ex-415, Reno 553; Reno 803 and Dism 12/15.

554 #5928 Ex-416, Reno 554; Reno 804 and Dism 12/15.

CLASS 124

4-6-0 Baldwin 1892 19x24" 67" 124,000# 17,586# TE

550 #12578 Orig RGW 61; Dism 1924.

551 #12596 Orig RGW 62; Dism 1924.

552 #12954 Orig RGW 66; weight 127,850#; Dism 1924.

CLASS C-14

2-8-0 Baldwin 1882 15x20" 36" 65,400# 14,343# TE

553 #6032 Orig 275; Sold to D&RGW Ry 7/12/86, then RGW 101 and rebuilt to standard gauge; Reno RGW 11; to D&RG 553; Reno 290; Dism 8/24.

CLASS 77

554-5 Orig RGW narrow gauge locomotives, converted to standard gauge; received by D&RG and subsequently reconverted to narrow gauge; see Narrow Gauge section, these numbers.

CLASS C-28

2-8-0 Baldwin 20x24" 46" 113,200# 24,900# TE 140# BP

555 #8950-1888 Reno 581, 1908; Reno 681; Dism 1945.

556 #8953-1888 Reno 636; Dism 5/36.

557 #8954-1888 Reno 637; Dism 8/25.

558 #8958-1888 Reno 638; Dism 10/29.

559 #8959-1888 Reno 639; Dism 12/28.

560 #9088-1888 Reno 640; Dism 12/26.

561 #9089-1888 Reno 641; Dism 1936.

562 #9090-1888 Reno 642; Dism 2/26.

563 #9093-1888 Dism 4/17.

564 #9094-1888 Reno 644; Dism 10/38.

565	#9619-1888	Reno 645; Dism 12/26.
566	#9617-1888	Reno 635; Dism 1/39.
567	#9620-1888	Dism 3/24.
568	#9626-1888	Dism 12/15.
569	#9745-1889	Reno 643; Dism 12/34.
570	#9747-1889	Reno 630; Dism 2/26.
571	#9751-1889	Reno 631; Dism 12/27.
572	#9752-1889	Reno 632; Dism 12/26.
573	#9754-1889	Reno 633; Sold to San Luis Valley Southern RR 104, 4/44; Dism.
574	#9755-1889	Reno 634; Dism 8/51.
575	#10395-1889	Dism 6/16.
576	#10396-1889	Reno 676; Dism 12/28.
577	#10397-1889	Reno 677; Dism 12/29.
578	#10398-1889	Reno 678; Dism 11/34.
579	#10401-1889	Reno 679; Dism 6/36.
580	#10481-1889	Reno 680; Dism 12/39.
581	#10480-1889	Sold 6/1903 to Colorado & Southeastern RR #1.
582	#11202-1890	Reno 682; Dism 5/36.
583	#11207-1890	Reno 683; Sold to San Luis Valley Southern RR 106, 5/47; Sold to Colorado Railroad Museum, 1962.
584	#11222-1890	Reno 684; Dism 10/29.
585	#11223-1890	Reno 685; Dism 6/36.
586	#11229-1890	Reno 686; Dism 12/26.
587	#11236-1890	Reno 687; Dism 12/27.
588	#11243-1890	Dism 8/20.
589	#11244-1890	Reno 689; Dism 3/26.
590	#11238-1890	Dism 3/24.
591	#11239-1890	Reno 691; Dism 10/38.
592	#11249-1890	Reno 648; Dism 12/26.
593	#11254-1890	Reno 657; Sold to San Luis Valley Southern RR 103, 8/29; Dism ca. 1945.
594	#11245-1890	Reno 671; Dism 12/39.
595	#11252-1890	Reno 668; Dism 12/28.
596	#11237-1890	Reno 688; Sold to San Luis Valley Southern RR 105, 1945; To parts; Dism 1977.
597	#11251-1890	Sold to Deep Creek RR 2, 12/16 or 6/17; Dism 1/39.
598	#11259-1890	Dism 4/17.
599	#11260-1890	Reno 690; Dism 10/38.
600	#11255-1890	Reno 670; Dism 4/41.
601	#11256-1890	Reno 661; Dism 6/36.
602	#11257-1890	Reno 672; Dism 10/38.
603	#11261-1890	Reno 673; Dism.
604	#11262-1890	Reno 674; Dism 1/35.
605	#11258-1890	Reno 675; Dism 12/27.
606	#11263-1890	Reno 646; Dism 12/39.
607	#11279-1890	Reno 647; Dism 12/29.
608	#11271-1890	Dism 2/16.
609	#11282-1890	Reno 649; Dism 6/36.
610	#11904-1891	Reno 650; Dism 10/29.
611	#11905-1891	Reno 651; Dism 5/36.
612	#11911-1891	Reno 652; Dism 1/35.
613	#11908-1891	Reno 653; Dism 12/39.
614	#11912-1891	Reno 654; Dism 1/39.
615	#11924-1891	Reno 655; Dism 12/34.
616	#12005-1891	Reno 656; Dism 11/27.
617	#12006-1891	Dism 4/17.
618	#12013-1891	Reno 658; Dism 10/34.
619	#12037-1891	Reno 659; Dism 11/34.
620	#12038-1891	Reno 660; Dism 11/34.
621	#12043-1891	Dism 8/20.
622	#12050-1891	Reno 662; Dism 5/36.
623	#12058-1891	Reno 663; Dism 12/39.
624	#12059-1891	Reno 664; Dism 12/26.
625	#12060-1891	Reno 665; Dism 5/36.
626	#12064-1891	Reno 666; Dism 12/28.
627	#12073-1891	Reno 667; Dism 12/26.
628	#12087-1891	Dism 6/16.
629	#12095-1891	Reno 669; Dism 10/29.

These engines were extensively shopped, and in later years had 160# boiler pressure, 115,000 to 120,000# engine weight, and 47″ or 50½″ drives with 27,780# or 25,600# tractive effort (respectively).

CLASS C-26

2-8-0 Baldwin 20x24″ 51″ 120,100# 25,600# TE 140# BP

630	#10270-1889	Orig RGW 111; Reno 600; Dism 10/29.
631	#10272-1889	Orig RGW 112; Reno 601; Dism 12/26.

(*Continued on Page 40*)

0-8-0T No. 10, the Burnham shop goat in the 1920's, had formerly been No. 800 (H.E. High photo). Class C-28 No. 681 works as the Leadville switcher in 1938. (Lamar M. Kelley) RGW class T-19 No. 70 (left-above) was built as a Vauclain compound (H.E. Broadbelt collection), while D&RG class T-26 No. 705, also built by Baldwin in 1898, was single expansion. (below, Colorado State Historical Society) C-26 No. 122 was in service at Stockton, California (left) during construction of the Western Pacific in the early 1900's. (A.M. Payne Collection)

RIO GRANDE WESTERN RY.
GREAT
SALT LAKE
ROUTE

632	#10273-1889	Orig RGW 113; Dism 2/24.
633	#10278-1889	Orig RGW 114; Dism 3/17.
634	#10279-1889	Orig RGW 115; Reno 604; Dism 10/29.
635	#10280-1889	Orig RGW 116; Reno 605; Sold to Victor Amer. Fuel Co., 7/51.
636	#10284-1889	Orig RGW 117; Reno 606; Dism 11/34.
637	#10285-1889	Orig RGW 118; Reno 607; Dism 12/34.
638	#10286-1889	Orig RGW 119; Dism 2/24.
639	#10289-1889	Orig RGW 120; Reno 625; Dism 8/24.
640	#10294-1889	Orig RGW 121; Reno 610; Dism 12/26.
641	#10384-1890	Orig RGW 122; Reno 611; Dism 10/29.
642	#10385-1890	Orig RGW 123; Reno 612; Dism 8/25.
643	#10386-1890	Orig RGW 124; Dism 3/17.
644	#10387-1890	Orig RGW 125; Dism 2/24.
645	#10388-1890	Orig RGW 126; Dism 2/24.
646	#10390-1890	Orig RGW 127; Reno 613; Dism 12/26.
647	#10391-1890	Orig RGW 128; Reno 603; Dism 1/28.
648	#10392-1890	Orig RGW 129; Dism 2/24.
649	#10393-1890	Orig RGW 130; Reno 609; Dism 3/26.
650	#10468-1890	Orig RGW 131; Reno 608; Dism 11/34.
651	#10471-1890	Orig RGW 132; Dism 1/16.
652	#10475-1890	Orig RGW 133; Reno 602; Dism 12/28.
653	#10476-1890	Orig RGW 134; Dism 3/17.
654	#10479-1890	Orig RGW 135; Reno 614; Dism 12/34.
655	#11585-1891	Orig RGW 136; Reno 615; Dism 10/29.
656	#11584-1891	Orig RGW 137; Reno 616; to List Constr. Co. 1927.
657	#11591-1891	Orig RGW 138; Reno 617; Dism 12/28.
658	#11592-1891	Orig RGW 139; Reno 618; Dism 12/34.
659	#11668-1891	Orig RGW 140; Reno 619; Dism 12/26.
660	#11669-1891	Orig RGW 141; Reno 620; Dism 10/29.
661	#11771-1891	Orig RGW 142; Sold Indian Valley RR. #1, 12/16.
662	#11777-1891	Orig RGW 143; Reno 626; Dism 8/24.
663	#12025-1891	Orig RGW 144; Reno 623; Dism 8/24.
664	#12026-1891	Orig RGW 145; Reno 624; Dism 8/24.
665	#12036-1891	Orig RGW 146; Dism 2/24.
666	#12033-1891	Orig RGW 147; Dism 2/24.
667	#12034-1891	Orig RGW 148; Dism 2/16.
668	#12417-1892	Orig RGW 149; Sold Indian Valley #2, 12/16; Dism 12/39.
669	#12421-1892	Orig RGW 150; Dism prior to 1924.
670	#12423-1892	Orig RGW 151; Reno 621; Dism 8/25.
671	#12431-1892	Orig RGW 152; Dism 2/24.
672	#12426-1892	Orig RGW 153; Reno 622; Dism 8/25.

Some of these engines later had 47″ drivers and 27,778# tractive effort. Specifications above are 1908 D&RG specifications.

CLASS C-16

2-8-0 Baldwin 1896 16x20″ 38″ 80,200# 16,600# TE 145# BP

680	#14875	Orig San Pete Valley RR 50, in service 9/25/12; Reno 287; Dism 8/24.
681	#14876	Orig San Pete Valley RR 52, in service 1/20/12; Reno 288; Dism 8/24.

CLASS T-26

4-6-0 Baldwin 20x26″ 63″ 149,065# 25,959# TE 200# BP*

700	#14989-1896	Reno 540; Dism 8/24.
701	#14990-1896	Reno 541; Dism 8/24.
702	*D&RG-1897	Reno 542; Dism 3/26.
703	*D&RG-1897	Reno 543; Dism 9/25.
704	#15692-1898	Reno 544; Dism 12/26.
705	#15693-1898	Reno 535; Dism 8/24.
706	#16178-1898	Reno 536; Dism 12/26.
707	#16179-1898	Reno 537; Dism 8/24.

 *702 and 703 were constructed by the D&RG RR.

708	#16180-1898	Reno 538; Dism 12/26.	710	#16182-1898	Reno 545; Dism 11/26.
709	#16181-1898	Reno 539; Dism 11/26.	711	#16183-1898	Reno 546; Dism 3/26.

CLASS T-19

4-6-0 Baldwin 19x24" 67" 134,000# 18,666# TE 170# BP

All originally 21 & 33x24" Vauclain Compound, 66" drivers. #713 180# BP and 19,785# TE.

712	#12601-1892	Orig RGW 63; Reno 521; Dism 8/24.	715	#15561-1898	Orig RGW 70; Reno 526; Dism 8/24.
713	#12946-1892	Orig RGW 64; Reno 520; Dism 8/24.	716	#15562-1898	Orig RGW 71; Reno 527; Dism 8/24.
714	#12950-1892	Orig RGW 65; Dism 8/24.	717	#15563-1898	Orig RGW 72; Reno 528; Dism 8/24.
			718	#15564-1898	Orig RGW 73; Reno 525; Dism 11/26.

CLASS T-28

4-6-0 Brooks 1899 20x26" 63" 168,700# 28,063# TE 200# BP

#730-739, 169,700# weight; all originally 21x26", 160,000# wt. and 32,487# TE.

720	#3196	Dism 12/26.	729	#3205	Dism 12/27.
721	#3197	Dism 12/26.	730	#3344	Dism 12/34.
722	#3198	Dism 12/26.	731	#3345	Dism 12/34.
723	#3199	Dism 12/26.	732	#3346	Dism 12/34.
724	#3200	Dism 12/27.	733	#3347	Dism 12/34.
725	#3201	Dism 12/27.	734	#3348	Dism 12/34.
726	#3202	Dism 12/28.	735	#3349	Dism 12/34.
727	#3203	Dism 12/27.	736	#3350	Dism 12/34.
728	#3204	Dism 12/27.	737	#3351	Dism 12/27.
			738	#3352	Dism 12/27.
			739	#3353	Dism 12/27.

CLASS T-24

4-6-0 Schenectady 1901 20x26" 67" 161,500# 24,400# TE 185# BP

Rebuilt 1906 from Compound 22 & 34x26".

740	#5724	Orig RGW 80; Reno 530; Dism 5/27.	742	#5726	Orig RGW 82; Reno 532; Dism 12/28.
741	#5725	Orig RGW 81; Reno 531; Dism 5/27.	743	#5727	Orig RGW 83; Reno 533; Dism 12/27.

CLASS T-29

4-6-0 Brooks 21x26" 67" 184,000# 29,093# TE 200# BP

#763,777 Reno 760,761 and rebuilt 63" drivers, 30,940# TE, Class T-31.

760	#45667-1908	Reno 763; Dism 1/39.	766	#45673-1908	Dism 1/37.
761	#45668-1908	Reno 777; Dism 10/38.	767	#45674-1908	Dism 11/39.
762	#45669-1908	Dism 2/48.	768	#45675-1908	Dism 7/36.
763	#45670-1908	Reno 760; Dism 1945.	769	#45676-1908	Dism 2/37.
764	#45671-1908	Dism 10/38.	770	#45683-1908	Dism 1/39.
765	#45672-1908	Dism 6/48.	771	#45684-1908	Dism 12/48.

(Continued on Page 43)

RIO GRANDE
GREAT
SALT LAKE
ROUTE
WESTERN RAILWAY

Three classes of American Locomotive Company ten wheelers are represented by RGW T-24 No. 82 (History Center, Schenectady), D&RG T-28 No. 723 (Colorado State Historical Society), and T-29 No. 784, the last 4-6-0 to survive on the roster, at Montrose in 1949 (Ross Grenard). At the bottom of the page are two stalwarts of the Salt Lake City switcher pool in the 1930's, the unique 2-6-0T shopgoat No. 578 (Otto Perry Collection –Denver Public Library) and S-33 0-6-0 No. 57. (Richard H. Kindig)

772	#45685-1908	Dism 11/39.
773	#45686-1908	Dism 2/51.
774	#45687-1908	Dism 11/39.
775	#46411-1909	Dism 3/42.
776	#46412-1909	Dism 2/48.
777	#46413-1909	Reno 761; Dism 3/41.
778	#46414-1909	Dism 3/26.
779	#46415-1909	Dism 3/49.
780	#46416-1909	Dism 5/42.
781	#46417-1909	Dism 3/42.
782	#46418-1909	Dism 3/41.
783	#46419-1909	Dism 1945.
784	#46420-1909	Dism 6/52.
785	#46421-1909	Dism 9/49.
786	#46422-1909	Dism 10/38.
787	#46423-1909	Dism 1/39.
788	#46424-1909	Dism 10/47.
789	#46425-1909	Dism 12/47.
790	#46426-1909	Dism 11/39.
791	#46427-1909	Dism 10/38.
792	#46428-1909	Dism 6/36.
793	#46429-1909	Dism 10/38.

CLASS S-23

0-6-0 Schenectady 1900 19x24" 51" 96,000# 23,104# TE 160# BP

805	#5629	Orig RGW 21; Reno 20; Dism 10/28.
806	#5638	Orig RGW 22; Reno 21; Dism 9/36.
807	#5635	Orig RGW 23; Reno 22; Dism 9/36.

CLASS G-20

2-6-0 Baldwin 18x24" 47" 102,750# 19,688# TE 140# BP

805	#11292-1890	Reno 827, 1908; Dism 3/24.
806	#11293-1890	Reno 828, 1908; Reno 578; to 2-6-0T, 1928; Dism 5/36.
807	#11296-1890	Reno 829, 1908; Dism 2/17.
808	#11297-1890	Dism 3/23.
809	#11302-1890	Dism 8/17.
810	#11300-1890	Dism 1/16.
811	#11312-1890	Dism 6/16.
812	#11446-1891	Dism 3/24.
813	#11447-1891	Dism 6/16.
814	#11450-1891	Sold 7/17 to Denver & Intermountain Ry. #1.
815	#11463-1891	Dism 6/16.
816	#11485-1891	Dism 6/16.
817	#11486-1891	Dism 2/24.
818	#11494-1891	Dism 6/16.
819	#11495-1891	Reno 579; Dism 3/26.
820	#11560-1891	Dism 6/16.
821	#11561-1891	Reno 575; Dism 12/28.
822	#11579-1891	Reno 577; Dism 8/24.
823	#11623-1891	Sold 7/17 to Denver & Intermountain Ry. #2.
824	#11624-1891	Dism 6/16.
825	#11881-1891	Dism 2/17.
826	#11886-1891	Reno 576; Dism 8/24.

CLASS S-33

0-6-0 Baldwin 20x26" 51" 150,000# 32,800# TE 190# BP

831	#29410-1906	Reno 50; Sold to Columbia Steel Co., Geneva, Utah, 11/43.
832	#29411-1906	Reno 51; Sold to U.S. Govt., Rocky Mtn. Arsenal #2, 12/42; out of service 12/44.
833	#29437-1906	Reno 52; Sold to U. S. Govt., Athol (Idaho) Naval Trng. Station, 12/42; Offered in War Assets Adm. Sale, Farragut, Idaho, 3/48.
834	#29438-1906	Reno 53; Sold to Columbia Steel Co., Geneva, Utah, 11/43.
835	#29450-1906	Reno 54; Sold to Dept. of Interior, Bur. of Reclamation, 12/42.
836	#30695-1907	Reno 55; Sold to Columbia Steel Co., Geneva, Utah, 9/43.

837	#30696-1907	Reno 56; Sold to Columbia Steel Co., Geneva, Utah, 3/43.
838	#30697-1907	Reno 57; Sold to Columbia Steel Co., Geneva, Utah, 7/43.
839	#30699-1907	Reno 58; Dism 7/52.
840	#30725-1907	Reno 59; Dism 8/52.

CLASS S-33 Schenectady

0-6-0 Schenectady 20"x26" 51" 150,000# 31,200#TE 180#BP

841	#46508-1909	Reno 60; Dism 7/44.
842	#46509-1909	Reno 61; Sold to Hayden Coal Co., 7/44.
843	#46510-1909	Reno 62; Dism 7/52.

CLASS C-41

2-8-0 Baldwin 1900 22x28" 54" 183,790# 40,531# TE 190# BP

901	#18180	Reno 951; Dism 6/36.
902	#18181	Reno 952; Dism 5/36.
903	#18182	Reno 953; Dism 6/36.
904	#18204	Reno 954; Dism 5/36.
905	#18205	Reno 955; Rebuilt 1937 to 2-8-0T #01; Dism 9/46.
906	#18216	Reno 956; Dism 11/46.
907	#18217	Reno 957; Dism 6/36.
908	#18218	Reno 958; Dism 1/37.
909	#18236	Reno 959; Dism 5/36.
910	#18237	Reno 960; Dism 5/36.
911	#18238	Reno 961; Dism 6/36.
912	#18239	Reno 962; Dism 6/36.
913	#18282	Reno 963; Dism 11/39.
914	#18283	Reno 964; Dism 11/39.
915	#18284	Reno 950; Dism 5/36.

CLASS C-39

2-8-0 Baldwin 1905 22x28" 56" 185,600# 39,083# TE 190# BP

916	#26006	Dism 5/36.
917	#26024	Dism 6/36.
918	#26039	Dism 6/36.
919	#26050	Dism 2/37.
920	#26069	Dism 6/36.
921	#26070	Dism 6/36.
922	#26102	Dism 1/39.
923	#26108	Dism 4/41.
924	#26154	Dism 9/36.
925	#26155	Dism 10/38.

CLASS G-28

2-6-0 Baldwin 1898 20x26" 61" 140,600# 27,535# TE 190# BP

940	#15578	Orig RGW 200; Reno 590; Dism 11/24.
941	#15579	Orig RGW 201; to Barry Equipment Co. 6/17.
942	#15580	Orig RGW 202; Reno 591; Dism 3/26.
943	#15581	Orig RGW 203; Sold to Wyoming Ry. 1/17.

CLASS G-28

2-6-0 Schenectady 1901 20x26" 61" 154,400# 27,535# TE 190# BP

Converted 7/07 from Compound 22½ & 35x26".

950	#5718	Orig RGW 500; Reno 596; Dism 12/27.
951	#5719	Orig RGW 501; Reno 597; Dism 10/28.
952	#5720	Orig RGW 502; Reno 592; Dism 3/26.
953	#5721	Orig RGW 503; Reno 593; Dism 3/26.
954	#5722	Orig RGW 504; Reno 594; Dism 12/29.
955	#5723	Orig RGW 505; Reno 595; Dism 1/37.

CLASS C-39

2-8-0 Baldwin 1912 21x26" 51" 172,600# 39,000# TE 190# BP

958 #38837 Orig Spring Canon Coal Co. #1; Reno 915; Dism 1/37.

CLASS C-38

2-8-0 Richmond 1900 22x28" 56" 183,000# 38,054# TE 185# BP

960 #3006 Orig RGW 300; Reno 900; Dism 7/36.

961 #3007 Orig RGW 301; Reno 901; Dism 9/36.

962 #3008 Orig RGW 302; Reno 902; Dism 5/36.

963 #3009 Orig RGW 303; Reno 903; Dism 6/36.

CLASS C-42

2-8-0 Richmond 1900 22x28" 51" 179,600# 41,785# TE 185# BP

970 #3002 Orig RGW 400; Dism 5/36.

971 #3003 Orig RGW 401; Dism 12/29.

972 #3004 Orig RGW 402; Dism 5/36.

973 #3005 Orig RGW 403; Dism 7/36.

CLASS C-40

2-8-0 Richmond 1901 21x30" 57" 199,000# 39,500# TE 200# BP

Converted 3/07 from Compound 17 & 28x30".

980 #3184 Orig RGW 600; Reno 940; Dism 6/36.

981 #3185 Orig RGW 601; Reno 941; Dism 7/36.

982 #3186 Orig RGW 602; Reno 942; Dism 7/36.

983 #3187 Orig RGW 603; Reno 943; Dism 6/36.

984 #3188 Orig RGW 604; Reno 944; Dism 6/36.

CLASS C-40

2-8-0 Baldwin 1901 21x30" 56" 199,000# 39,500# TE 200# BP

Converted 3/07 from Compound 17 & 28x30".

990 #18761 Orig RGW 700; Reno 930; Dism 1945.

991 #18762 Orig RGW 701; Reno 931; Dism 1945.

992 #18778 Orig RGW 702; Reno 932; Dism 1946.

993 #18779 Orig RGW 703; Reno 933; Dism 1945.

994 #18780 Orig RGW 704; Reno 934; Dism 1945.

CLASS T-31

4-6-0 Baldwin 1902 21x26" 63" 178,600# 30,950# TE 200# BP

Converted from Compound 15½ & 26x26" and 28,500# TE; #757 had 66" drivers and 29,600# TE.

1001 #20381 Reno 750, 1908; Dism 6/36.

1002 #20382 Reno 751, 1908; Dism 5/36.

1003 #20383 Reno 752, 1908; Dism 7/36.

1004 #20404 Reno 753, 1908; Dism 1/39.

1005 #20405 Reno 754, 1908; Dism 6/36.

1006 #20411 Reno 755, 1908; Dism 5/36.

1007 #20412 Reno 756, 1908; Dism 3/26.

1008 #20429 Reno 757, 1908; Dism 5/36.

1009 #20430 Reno 758, 1908; Dism 6/36.

1010 #20431 Reno 759, 1908; Dism 3/26.

CLASS P-44

4-6-2 Baldwin 1913 26x26" 67" 261,080# 44,594# TE 200# BP

All originally 185# BP and 41,200# TE; later 190# BP and 42,370# TE.

(Continued on Page 48)

RGW C-42 No. 401 was big power for its day, built to handle the four percent grade of Soldier Summit. (top, History Center, Schenectady) Also a Richmond graduate of 1900, the 900 rests in the Salt Lake City dead line in 1934 (G.M. Best). G-28 Mogul No. 943, formerly RGW No. 203, is stored in Denver in 1917. (Otto Perry photo, Western History Collection, Denver Public Library) C-39 No. 915 had started life as Spring Canon Coal Co. No. 1 (G.M. Best). No. 60 was a well maintained switcher at Pueblo in 1936 (Otto Perry photo, Western History Collection, Denver Public Library). The 601 was another Richmond product, built as a compound. (History Center, Schenectady)

Still more 900's—C-40 No. 933 at Salida in 1936 (Otto Perry photo, Western History Collection, Denver Public Library) and C-41 No. 964 at Burnham. (H.E. High photo, Richard H. Kindig Collection)

The 916 is pictured south of Denver in 1906, when barely a year old (left, Railway & Locomotive Historical Society Collection). No. 01, nee 955, replaced No. 578 as the Salt Lake City shop goat in 1937. (J.C. Thode) No. 1007 was a fine looking compound posed for its builder's photo in Philadelphia (H.L. Broadbelt Collection)

1001	#39144	Reno 801; Dism 9/53.
1002	#39145	Reno 802; Dism 10/49.
1003	#39146	Reno 803; Dism 5/50.
1004	#39147	Reno 804; Dism 8/53.
1005	#39148	Reno 805; Dism 12/49.
1006	#39149	Reno 800; Dism 7/52.

CLASS C-41

2-8-0 Baldwin 1902 21x30" 55" 182,000# 40,893# TE 200# BP

Originally Compound 17 & 28x28#, 183,920# wt. and 43,200# TE.

1101	#20519	Reno 1001; Dism 8/44.
1102	#20520	Reno 1002; Dism 9/52.
1103	#20521	Reno 1003; Rblt 1930 to narrow gauge #497.
1104	#20522	Reno 1004; Rblt 1928 to narrow gauge #495.
1105	#20550	Reno 1005; Rblt 1928 to narrow gauge #493.
1106	#20609	Reno 1006; Dism 8/44.
1107	#20610	Reno 1007; Dism 1945.
1108	#20611	Reno 1008; Dism 2/37.
1109	#20640	Reno 1009; Rblt 1930 to narrow gauge #498.
1110	#20641	Reno 1010; Dism 8/44.
1111	#20666	Reno 1011; Dism 8/44.
1112	#20667	Reno 1012; Dism 8/44.
1113	#20668	Reno 1013; to 0-8-0 at Salt Lake City, 1937; Dism 5/44.
1114	#20695	Reno 1014; Rblt 1928 to narrow gauge #490.
1115	#20696	Reno 1015; Dism 3/47.
1116	#20697	Reno 1016; Dism 3/49.
1117	#20698	Reno 1017; Dism 2/37.
1118	#20746	Reno 1018; Dism 1/37.
1119	#20747	Reno 1019; Dism 1945.
1120	#20748	Reno 1020; Rblt 1928 to nar row gauge #494.
1121	#20749	Reno 1021; Rblt 1928 to narrow gauge #492.
1122	#20750	Reno 1022; Dism 1946.
1123	#20751	Reno 1023; Rblt 1930 to narrow gauge #496.
1124	#20752	Reno 1024; Dism 7/50.
1125	#20753	Reno 1025; Rblt 1930 to narrow gauge #499.
1126	#20829	Reno 1026; Rblt 1928 to narrow gauge #491.
1127	#20830	Reno 1027; Dism 1945.
1128	#20831	Reno 1028; Dism 3/49.
1129	#20872	Reno 1029; Dism 1945.
1130	#20873	Reno 1000; Dism 6/48.

CLASS C-48

2-8-0 Schenectady 24x28" 57" 220,400# 48,100# TE 200# BP

Originally 23x28", 216,000#, 190# BP and 42,000# TE. Rebuilt as above with 44,000# TE until superheated.

1131	#39013-1906	Dism 10/47.
1132	#39014-1906	Dism 4/52.
1133	#39015-1906	Dism 8/50.
1134	#39016-1906	Dism 9/56.
1135	#39017-1906	Dism 2/48.
1136	#39018-1906	Dism 12/56.
1137	#39019-1906	Dism 10/56.
1138	#39020-1906	Dism 12/56.
1139	#39021-1906	Dism 11/56.
1140	#39022-1906	Dism 5/55.
1141	#39328-1906	Dism 12/47.
1142	#39329-1906	Dism 10/55.
1143	#39330-1906	Sold Geneva Steel Div. 1/9/56.
1144	#39331-1906	Dism 5/55.
1145	#39332-1906	Dism 1946.
1146	#39333-1906	Dism 5/55.
1147	#39334-1906	Dism 12/47.
1148	#39335-1906	Dism 10/55.
1149	#39336-1906	Dism 3/49.
1150	#39337-1906	Dism 9/47.
1151	#44947-1908	Dism 12/56.
1152	#44920-1908	Dism 6/47.
1153	#44921-1908	Dism 1/55.
1154	#44922-1908	Dism 6/54.
1155	#44923-1908	Dism 3/49.

1156	#44924-1908	Dism 4/52.
1157	#44925-1908	Dism 5/55.
1158	#44926-1908	Dism 10/47.
1159	#44927-1908	Dism 5/55.
1160	#44928-1908	Dism 6/54.
1161	#44929-1908	Dism 12/56.
1162	#44930-1908	Dism 3/49.
1163	#44931-1908	Dism 12/56.
1164	#44932-1908	Dism 8/48.
1165	#44933-1908	Dism 7/50.
1166	#44934-1908	Dism 4/56.
1167	#44935-1908	Dism 11/56.
1168	#44936-1908	Dism 12/51.
1169	#44937-1908	Dism 10/56.
1170	#44938-1908	Dism 1946.
1171	#44939-1908	Dism 7/54.
1172	#44940-1908	Dism 12/48.
1173	#44941-1908	Dism 12/56.
1174	#44942-1908	Dism 2/55.
1175	#44943-1908	Dism 12/56.
1176	#44944-1908	Dism 3/49.
1177	#44945-1908	Dism 12/56.
1178	#44946-1908	Dism 2/55.

Nos. 1180-1199 following originally RGW, same numbers.

1180	#40125-1906	Sold Geneva Steel Div. 1/9/56.
1181	#40126-1906	Dism 10/49.
1182	#40127-1906	Dism 8/53.
1183	#40128-1906	Dism 8/53.
1184	#40129-1906	Dism 9/56.
1185	#40130-1906	Dism 12/56.
1186	#40131-1906	Dism 7/54.
1187	#40132-1906	Dism 4/49.
1188	#40133-1906	Dism 3/50.
1189	#40134-1906	Dism 6/55.
1190	#40522-1906	Dism 4/50.
1191	#40523-1906	Dism 7/54.
1192	#40524-1906	Dism 9/56.
1193	#40525-1906	Dism 7/54.
1194	#40526-1906	Dism 11/56.
1195	#40527-1906	Dism 10/56.
1196	#40528-1906	Dism 6/55.
1197	#40529-1906	Dism 6/54.
1198	#40530-1906	Dism 1/55.
1199	#40531-1906	Dism 2/55.

CLASS K-59

2-8-2 Baldwin 1912 27x30" 63" 276,000# 59,000# TE 200# BP

Originally 170# BP and 50,200# TE; later 185# BP and 54,587# TE.

1200	#38772	Dism 7/54.
1201	#38773	Dism 9/38.
1202	#38774	Dism 6/55.
1203	#38775	Dism 12/48.
1204	#38776	Dism 7/50.
1205	#38777	Dism 2/55.
1206	#38778	Dism 3/48.
1207	#38779	Dism 9/56.
1208	#38780	Dism 8/52.
1209	#38781	Dism 6/55.
1210	#38870	Dism 7/49.
1211	#38871	Dism 6/48.
1212	#38872	Dism 6/50.
1213	#38873	Dism 2/55.

CLASS F-81

2-10-2 Brooks 1916 31x32" 63" 428,500# 81,200# TE 195# BP

Placed in service 2/1917.

1250	#56620	Reno 1400; Dism 10/55.
1251	#56621	Reno 1401; Dism 10/55.
1252	#56622	Reno 1402; Dism 5/55.
1253	#56623	Reno 1403; Dism 2/55.
1254	#56624	Reno 1404; Dism 7/54.
1255	#56625	Reno 1405; Dism 5/55.
1256	#56626	Reno 1406; Dism 5/55.
1257	#56627	Reno 1407; Dism 5/55.
1258	#56628	Reno 1408; Dism 7/52.
1259	#56629	Reno 1409; Dism 7/52.

Definitely out of their milieu on a mountain railroad were the six P-44 Pacifics. Nevertheless, they served usefully for many years on a variety of passenger hauls, often double headed with 1200 series 2-8-2's. No. 804 is at Colorado Springs in 1941. Equally out of place, but also turning in many years of good service, were their diesel era counterparts, the six Alco PA's. (Richard H. Kindig)

C-48 2-8-0 No. 1141 has just emerged from the Schenectady Works of its builder in 1906 (above). 1100's did yeoman service all over the system until the final run of standard gauge steam on the Rio Grande, made by No. 1151 on December 26, 1956. (History Center, Schenectady). *C-41 No. 1013 was a one-of-a-kind 0-8-0 conversion at Salt Lake City in 1938.* (above right, G.M. Best photo, Richard H. Kindig Collection)

The dual service 1200 series 2-8-2's (above) were equipped with smoke deflectors in the 1930's for Moffat Tunnel route service. The 1400's (left) were the only D&RGW ten-coupled power and, other than a few C-41 2-8-0's, had the road's only cylindrical type tenders. They served mainly on the Salt Lake Division (both, Richard H. Kindig)

Originally dual service locomotives, but used mainly on freight hauls, the hefty 1500's came in three sizes. Booster equipped 1511-1520 developed a mighty 79000 pounds tractive effort. Class M-69 (below) was a war time purchase from the Norfolk & Western, No. 1552 at Helper in 1947 being ex-N&W 208. (top and bottom, Richard H. Kindig; left above, H.K. Vollrath Collection; left below, John W. Maxwell)

CLASS M-67

4-8-2 Brooks 1922 28x30" 63" 377,000# 66,640# TE 210# BP

1501	#63307	Dism 7/54.	1506	#63312	Dism 9/53.
1502	#63308	Dism 1/52.	1507	#63313	Dism 2/52.
1503	#63309	Dism 4/52.	1508	#63314	Dism 4/52.
1504	#63310	Dism 7/54.	1509	#63315	Dism 10/55.
1505	#63311	Dism 6/50.	1510	#63316	Dism 1/55.

CLASS M-78

4-8-2 Brooks 1923 28x30" 63" 384,200# 66,640# TE 210# BP

78,967# TE with booster.

			1515	#64292	Dism 4/52.
1511	#64288	Dism 3/52.	1516	#64293	Dism 6/54.
1512	#64289	Dism 2/55.	1517	#64294	Dism 9/53.
1513	#64290	Dism 11/53.	1518	#64295	Dism 7/54.
1514	#64291	Dism 4/52.	1519	#64296	Dism 10/55.
			1520	#64297	Dism 7/52.

CLASS M-67

4-8-2 Brooks 1923 28x30" 63" 378,600# 66,640# TE 210# BP

1521	#64687	Dism 10/53.	1526	#64692	Dism 10/55.
1522	#64688	Dism 2/55.	1527	#64693	Dism 5/55.
1523	#64689	Dism 1/52.	1528	#64694	Dism 2/52.
1524	#64690	Dism 8/49.	1529	#64695	Dism 5/55.
1525	#64691	Dism 12/49.	1530	#64696	Dism 5/50.

CLASS M-69

4-8-2 Roanoke 1926 28x30" 63" 401,900# 68,800# TE

1550	#241	Sold 4/48.
1551	#242	Sold 4/48.
1552	#243	Sold 5/48.
1553	#244	Sold 5/48.

Orig Norfolk & Western 206-209, Class K-3; Purchased 5/45; Sold to Wheeling & Lake Erie Ry. Co. 6807-6810, then Nickel Plate 6807-6810, Class J-1; Sched. to be Reno 847-850 in 1951-52, but scrapped instead; 1551 Dism 2/53, others 11/52.

CLASS M-75

4-8-2 Baldwin 1926 (3) 25x30" 67" 419,310# 74,970# TE 210# BP

1600	#59240	Dism 4/49.	1605	#59293	Dism 9/49.
1601	#59241	Dism 12/41.	1606	#59294	Dism 7/49.
1602	#59242	Dism 9/49.	1607	#59295	Dism 11/49.
1603	#59243	Dism 4/49.	1608	#59336	Dism 6/48.
1604	#59244	Dism 3/48.	1609	#59337	Dism 6/48.

CLASS M-64

4-8-4 Baldwin 1929 27x30" 70" 418,150# 63,700# TE 240# BP

1700	#60712	Dism 6/56.	1702	#60714	Dism 6/54.
1701	#60713	Dism 6/56.	1703	#60715	Dism 1/55.

1704	#60716	Dism 2/55.	1709	#60721	Dism 6/56.
1705	#60717	Dism 6/54.	1710	#60920	Dism 3/55.
1706	#60718	Dism 7/52.	1711	#60921	Dism 9/52.
1707	#60719	Dism 6/50.	1712	#60922	Dism 1/55.
1708	#60720	Dism 6/50.	1713	#60923	Dism 10/55.

CLASS M-68

4-8-4 Baldwin 1937 26x30" 73" 470,000# 67,200# TE 285# BP

1800	#62130	Dism 8/54.	1803	#62133	Dism 8/52.
1801	#62131	Dism 10/53.	1804	#62134	Dism 6/54.
1802	#62132	Dism 10/53.			

CLASS L-62

2-6-6-2 Schenectady 1910 20½ & 33x32" 57" 340,000# 62,026# TE 200# BP

1050	#46717	Reno 3300; Dism 7/50.	1054	#46721	Reno 3304; Dism 10/47.
1051	#46718	Reno 3301; Dism 7/50.	1055	#46722	Reno 3305; Dism 1946.
1052	#46719	Reno 3302; Dism 8/52.	1056	#46723	Reno 3306; Dism 3/51.
1053	#46720	Reno 3303; Dism 10/50.	1057	#46724	Reno 3307; Dism 1946.

CLASS L-96

2-8-8-2 Schenectady 1913 26 & 40x32" 57" 458,000# 95,000# TE 200# BP

Nos. 3400, 3409 and 3414 (1941) and Nos. 3401-3 (1943) were reboilered, wt. of engine 482,500#. Between 1939 and 1945 the old slide valves were replaced by piston valves.

1060	#52038	Reno 3400; Dism 5/52.	1067	#52045	Reno 3407; Dism 5/50.
1061	#52039	Reno 3401; Dism 6/50.	1068	#52046	Reno 3408; Dism 4/51.
1062	#52040	Reno 3402; Dism 8/48.	1069	#52047	Reno 3409; Dism 11/51.
1063	#52041	Reno 3403; Dism 8/50.	1070	#52048	Reno 3410; Dism 4/50.
1064	#52042	Reno 3404; Dism 9/51.	1071	#52049	Reno 3411; Dism 1946.
1065	#52043	Reno 3405; Dism 3/51.	1072	#52050	Reno 3412; Dism 10/44.
1066	#52044	Reno 3406; Dism 6/50.	1073	#52051	Reno 3413; Dism 5/50.
			1074	#52052	Reno 3414; Dism 2/50.
			1075	#52053	Reno 3415; Dism 7/47.

CLASS L-76

2-6-6-2 Schenectady 1916 22 & 35x32" 57" 427,000# 75,830# TE

3350 #56459 Orig Norfolk & Western 1453; Purch. 8/43; Dism 7/52.

3351 #56460 Orig Norfolk & Western 1457; Purch. 8/43; Dism 5/50.

CLASS L-107

2-8-8-2 Richmond 1923 25 & 39x32" 57" 534,000# 107,374# TE 210# BP

3500	#64298	Dism 10/51.	3505	#64303	Dism 1/47.
3501	#64299	Dism 9/51.	3506	#64304	Dism 4/50.
3502	#64300	Dism 1/47.	3507	#64305	Dism 1/47.
3503	#64301	Dism 7/50.	3508	#64306	Dism 6/51.
3504	#64302	Dism 6/51.	3509	#64307	Dism 4/49.

Three successive versions of big dual service power on the Rio Grande in the years from 1926 to 1938 were the 1600's, 1700's and 1800's. (top and bottom, Richard H. Kindig; center, Ross Grenard)

Alco-Schenectady delivered the first D&RG Mallets in 1910. The 1057 was renumbered 3307 in 1924. (History Center, Schenectady) The L-96 Class 2-8-8-2's came three years later. The 3404 is at Helper, Utah, in June 1947. (Richard H. Kindig) No. 3351 had been Norfolk & Western 1457, purchased during World War II for Utah mine run service. (Richard H. Kindig)

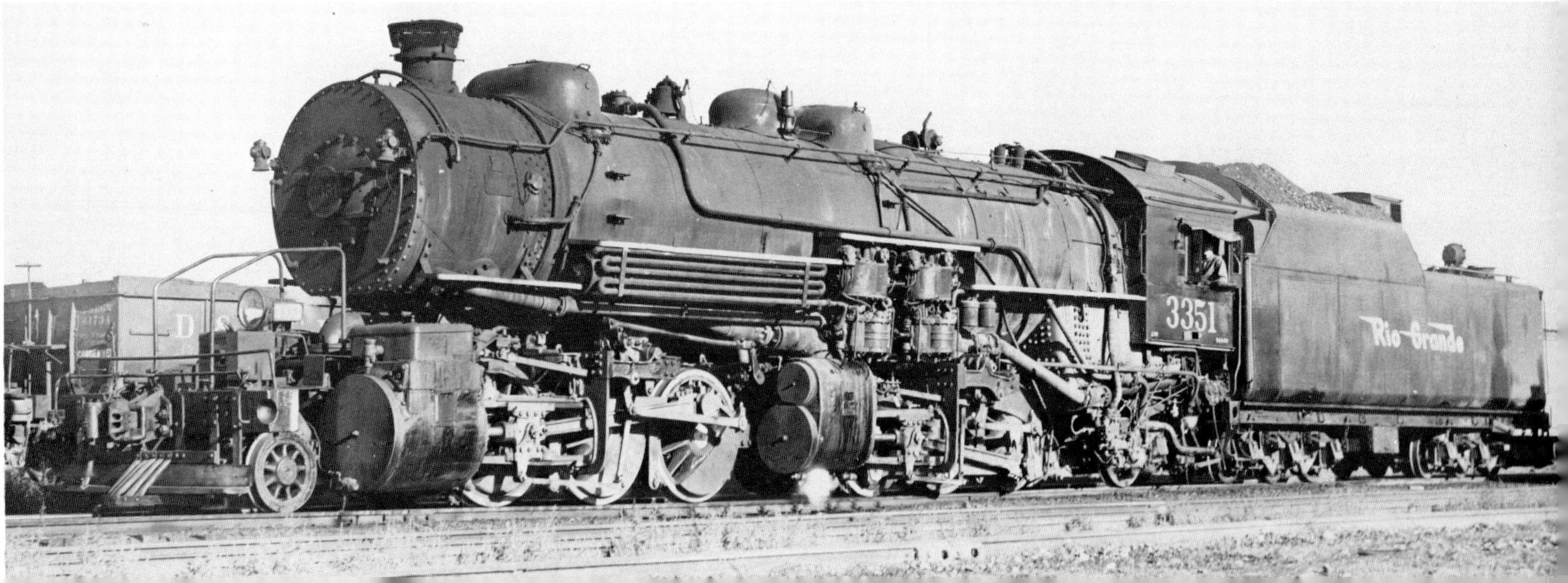

Articulated 2-8-8-2's ruled the Rio Grande's stable of steam freight power for a quarter century. Compound class L-107 3500's (top) worked Soldier Summit for years, while 3550's (above) were acquired from the Norfolk & Western late in World War II to serve as helpers on the Moffat Tunnel Route, Tennessee Pass and Soldier Summit. Simple classes L-131 and L-132 (below) roamed the entire system. (all—Richard H. Kindig)

CLASS L-109

2-8-8-2 25 & 39x32" 56" 526,000# 109,292# TE 240# BP

Former Norfolk & Western Class Y2, purchased in May, 1945.

3550	Roanoke	#225	1918	Orig N&W 1701; Dism 9/47.
3551	Baldwin	#51937	1919	Orig N&W 1722; Dism 3/49.
3552	Baldwin	#52317	1919	Orig N&W 1724; Dism 3/50.
3553	Baldwin	#52469	1919	Orig N&W 1728; Dism 3/49.
3554	Baldwin	#52676	1919	Orig N&W 1729; Dism 7/49.
3555	Baldwin	#52707	1919	Orig N&W 1730; Dism 4/49.
3556	Roanoke	#234	1924	Orig N&W 1710; Dism 7/48.
3557	Baldwin	#52351	1919	Orig N&W 1727; Dism 9/47.
3558	Roanoke	#230	1924	Orig N&W 1706; Dism 4/49.
3559	Roanoke	#233	1924	Orig N&W 1709; Dism 12/47.
3560	Baldwin	#51514	1919	Orig N&W 1713; Dism 9/47.
3561	Baldwin	#51557	1919	Orig N&W 1714; Dism 9/47.
3562	Baldwin	#51866	1919	Orig N&W 1719; Dism 3/51.
3563	Baldwin	#52318	1919	Orig N&W 1725; Dism 2/48.
3564	Baldwin	#52319	1919	Orig N&W 1726; Dism 9/47.

CLASS L-131

2-8-8-2 Brooks 1927 26x32" 63" 649,000# 131,800# TE 240# BP

3600	#67320	Dism 10/55.	3605	#67325	Dism 5/56.
3601	#67321	Dism 9/56.	3606	#67326	Dism 4/56.
3602	#67322	Dism 5/56.	3607	#67327	Dism 4/56.
3603	#67323	Dism 10/55.	3608	#67328	Dism 4/56.
3604	#67324	Dism 10/56.	3609	#67329	Dism 11/56.

CLASS L-132

2-8-8-2 Schenectady 1930 26x32" 63" 665,000# 131,800# TE

3610	#68328	Dism 3/56.	3615	#68333	Dism 3/56.
3611	#68329	Dism 3/56.	3616	#68334	Dism 10/56.
3612	#68330	Dism 11/56.	3617	#68335	Dism 10/55.
3613	#68331	Dism 5/56.	3618	#68336	Dism 10/55.
3614	#68332	Dism 10/55.	3619	#68337	Dism 11/56.

CLASS L-105

4-6-6-4 Baldwin 1938 23x32" 70" 620,000# 105,000# TE 255# BP

3700	#62139	Dism 3/56.	3705	#62144	Dism 3/51.
3701	#62140	Dism 10/51.	3706	#62145	Dism 4/51.
3702	#62141	Dism 4/51.	3707	#62146	Dism 11/51.
3703	#62142	Wrecked in boiler explosion, 10/19/52; Dism 6/55.	3708	#62147	Dism 2/56.
3704	#62143	Dism 9/51.	3709	#62148	Dism 12/51.

The peak of steam power development was reached with the L-105 4-6-6-4's delivered by Baldwin in 1938 and 1942. These two are shown at Helper, Utah, in 1947. An additional six 4-6-6-4's were diverted from the Union Pacific in 1943 via a lease from the War Production Board. Photographs of this class are extremely rare, but No. 3800 had its portrait taken in Salt Lake City on July 1, 1946, awaiting sale to the Clinchfield Railroad in faraway Tennessee. (top, Richard H. Kindig; others, Richard H. Kindig Collection)

Believe it or not, the D&RGW owned seven shays, including Nos. 1-5 inherited from Utah's Copper Belt. Although pictured in the 1930's, No. 5's cab was still lettered "RGW Y-33". (Richard H. Kindig Collection)

CLASS L-105

4-6-6-4 Baldwin 1942 23x32″ 70″ 641,700# 105,000# TE

3710	#64178	Dism 10/55.	3713	#64181	Dism 9/54.
3711	#64179	Dism 2/56.	3714	#64182	Dism 9/51.
3712	#64180	Dism 2/56.			

CLASS L-97

4-6-6-4 Schenectady 1943 21x32″ 69″ 627,000# 97,350# TE 280# BP

3800	#70163	3803	#70166
3801	#70164	3804	#70167
3802	#70165	3805	#70168

Leased from the Defense Plant Corporation (War Production Board). Delivered May & June, 1943; Sold to Clinchfield RR 670-675 in 1947; Dism about 1963.

Shay Geared Locomotives

The following seven shays were in use on the Copper Belt and the Kenilworth & Helper railways. The Copper Belt engines were relettered Rio Grande, but retained their original numbers.

No.	*Class*	*Bldr.*	*No., Date*	*Cyls.*	*Dr.*	*Wt.*	*T.E.*
CB 1	Y-21	Lima	598-1900	12½x12″	32″	135,400#	21,130#
CB 2	Y-25	Lima	843-1904	12x15″	32″	150,200#	25,180#
CB 3	Y-32	Lima	761-1904	14½x15″	40″	200,000#	31,800#
CB 4	Y-33	Lima	1585-1905	14½x15″	40″	200,000#	32,730#
CB 5	Y-33	Lima	1801-1906	14½x15″	40″	200,000#	32,730#
K&H 150	Y-40	Lima	2434-1911	14½x15″	36″	203,000#	40,397#
K&H 151	Y-40	Lima	2703-1913	14½x15″	36″	203,000#	40,397#

All of the above locomotives were of standard Lima three cylinder, three truck pattern, and weights given are total weights, including tender and third truck, loaded and in working order.

NOTES

1 — Orig Salt Lake & Mercur RR #7, then Copper Belt #1. To Morse Bros. Machinery Co., Denver; to Utah Construction Co., Guernsey, Wyo., then Morse Bros. 9/24 and scrapped.

2 — Orig Copper Belt #2. To Morse Bros. Machinery Co.; to McGoldrick Lumber Co., Spokane, Wash., then Morse Bros. 6/26 and scrapped.

3 — Orig Copper Belt #3. Scrapped 12/34.

4 — Orig Copper Belt #4. Scrapped 3/26.

5 — Orig Copper Belt #5. Scrapped 5/36.

150— Orig Kenilworth & Helper (Independent Coal & Coke Co.) #150. To Pacific Equipment Co., Portland, Ore., 6/29; to Hutchinson Logging Co. #90, South Beach, Ore., 8/29; to Alaska Junk Co., Portland, 4/36 and scrapped 1/40.

151— Orig Kenilworth & Helper (Independent Coal & Coke Co.) #151. To Pacific Equipment Co., Portland, 9/28; to Montborne Lumber Co., Big Lake, Wash., 4/29; scrapped 10/37, boiler to Willapoint Oyster Co., Bay Center, Wash.

795
795
Rio Grande

Rio Grande
Rio Grande

MOFFAT TUNNEL

1225
1225
Rio Grande

MOFFAT ENGINES

Moffat Road No. 302 served for only a few months in 1948 as D&RGW No. 795 before being scrapped. The 1229 (ex-D&SL 409) was the last Moffat engine to see service, lasting almost to the end of standard gauge steam in late 1956. No. 1225 was a rara avis in Rocky Mountain railroading – a product of the Lima Locomotive Works. On this page are DNW&P No. 112 when ready for delivery at Schenectady in August 1910 and the last of the famous Moffat Mallets at Hot Sulphur Springs, Colorado, in 1939. A few years later this engine was renumbered D&RGW 3375. (opposite center, Ross Grenard; above, History Center, Schenectady; others, Richard H. Kindig)

Denver & Salt Lake Locomotives

With the merger of the Denver & Salt Lake in 1947, the Rio Grande acquired a large number of elderly locomotives. New numbers were assigned to these locomotives, as shown in the chart below, and most were renumbered during 1948. The bulk of the locomotives, however, were taken from service and scrapped within two or three years, with the exception of a few 2-8-0s and 2-8-2s which lasted until the mid-1950s. Mechanical data, as compiled by Richard H. Kindig, follows the renumbering chart.

D&RGW No.	*D&SL No.*	*Class*	*Type*	*Builder*	*No.*	*Date*	*Date Dism.*
795	302	33	4-6-0	Schenectady	41616	11/1907	7/1948
796*	303	34	4-6-0	Schenectady	48147	7/1910	7/1948
1031	111	44	2-8-0	Schenectady	45579	10/1908	12/1951
1032*	112	44	2-8-0	Schenectady	48148	8/1910	12/1948
1033	113	44	2-8-0	Schenectady	48149	8/1910	7/1950
1034	118	44	2-8-0	Schenectady	48245	8/1910	5/1955
1035	119	44	2-8-0	Schenectady	48246	8/1910	5/1955
1036	120	44	2-8-0	Schenectady	48247	8/1910	5/1951
1037	121	44	2-8-0	Schenectady	48248	8/1910	12/1951
1038*	122	44	2-8-0	Schenectady	48249	8/1910	4/1948
1039	123	44	2-8-0	Schenectady	48250	8/1910	3/1951
1220	400	63	2-8-2	Lima	5100	1915	10/1953
1221	401	63	2-8-2	Lima	5101	1915	4/1949
1222	402	63	2-8-2	Lima	5102	1915	6/1954
1223	403	63	2-8-2	Lima	5103	1915	12/1948
1224	404	63	2-8-2	Lima	5104	1915	9/1956
1225	405	63	2-8-2	Lima	5105	1915	1/1955
1226	406	63	2-8-2	Lima	5106	1915	4/1952
1227	407	63	2-8-2	Lima	5107	1915	10/1953
1228	408	63	2-8-2	Schenectady	55984	8/1916	5/1952
1229	409	63	2-8-2	Schenectady	55985	8/1916	10/1956
3360	200	76	2-6-6-0	Schenectady	45604	10/1908	6/1949
3361	201	76	2-6-6-0	Schenectady	46560	10/1909	6/1952
3362*	202	76	2-6-6-0	Schenectady	46561	10/1909	12/1947
3363	203	76	2-6-6-0	Schenectady	48151	7/1910	8/1949
3364	204	76	2-6-6-0	Schenectady	48230	7/1910	8/1949
3365	205	76	2-6-6-0	Schenectady	48231	7/1910	8/1949
3366	206	76	2-6-6-0	Schenectady	48232	7/1910	7/1951
3367	207	76	2-6-6-0	Schenectady	48233	7/1910	5/1950
3368	208	76	2-6-6-0	Schenectady	48234	7/1910	8/1950
3369	209	76	2-6-6-0	Schenectady	48235	7/1910	4/1951
3370	211	76	2-6-6-0	Schenectady	53293	4/1913	7/1951
3371	212	76	2-6-6-0	Schenectady	55986	9/1916	4/1951
3372	213	76	2-6-6-0	Schenectady	55987	9/1916	7/1949
3373	214	76	2-6-6-0	Schenectady	55988	9/1916	7/1950
3374	215	76	2-6-6-0	Schenectady	55989	9/1916	7/1949
3375	216	76	2-6-6-0	Schenectady	56296	9/1916	7/1951

*Number assigned but not applied before scrapping.

CLASS D&SL	D&RGW	Cyl.	Dr.	Wt. Eng.	T.E.
33	T-33	20x28″	57″	189,000#	33,405#
34	Not assigned	20x28″	63″	165,000	34,150
44	C-43	22x28″	55″	219,000	43,980
63	K-63	26x30″	55″	295,000	62,700
76	L-77	21&33½x32″	55″	362,000	76,400

(Nos. 200-209 originally built as 0-6-6-0, rebuilt to 2-6-6-0)

In addition, the following D&SL locomotives were disposed of prior to the Rio Grande merger:

D&SL No.	Class	Type	Builder & No.	Date	Disp.
390, 391	19	4-4-0	Pittsburgh 1951, 1952	1899	Orig. Chesapeake Beach Ry. 3, 4; Dism 7/37.
20, 21	28	0-6-0	Schenectady 29038, 29039	7/1903	Dism 10/39.
300	30	4-6-0	Schenectady 29203	2/1904	Dism 4/47.
301	33	4-6-0	Schenectady 37708	5/1905	Dism 6/42.
100-102	42	2-8-0	Schenectady 29204-5, 37709	2/1904, 5/1905	Dism 5/37.
103-105	44	2-8-0	Schenectady 39947-9	5/1906	Dism 5/37.
106-107	44	2-8-0	Schenectady 41617-8	11/1906	Dism 10/39, 5/37.
108-110	44	2-8-0	Schenectady, 45576-8	10/1908	Dism 6/42, 8/43, 9/47.
114	44	2-8-0	Schenectady 48150	8/1910	Dism 6/42.
115-117	44	2-8-0	Schenectady 48242-4	8/1910	Sold to Columbia Steel Corp., Geneva, UT, 9, 11 & 10/42.
210	76	2-6-6-0	Schenectady 53292	4/1913	Destroyed 12/5/24.

CLASS 19	18x24″	60″	108,000	19,280
CLASS 28	19x26″	51″	132,000	28,160
CLASS 30	20x28″	63″	186,000	30,220
CLASS 42	22x28″	57″	209,500	42,420

Twenty-nine years of locomotive progress on the Denver & Rio Grande is represented by this turn of the century Denver yard scene with the tiny 2-4-0 narrow gauge UTE posed alongside No. 904, which was mammoth power for its time. Both engines proudly wore the inscription "Baldwin Locomotive Works Philadelphia U.S.A." (Richard H. Kindig Collection)

Diesel Locomotives of the Rio Grande

The Scenic Line's first diesel locomotive was a single 1000 horsepower, NW2 switcher purchased from the Electro-Motive Corporation, a firm which would be the Electro-Motive Division of General Motors before the number 7000 was delivered on January 22, 1941. That road number was chosen because it was far above that of any existing Rio Grande steam engine, the highest at the time being 3709, to avoid any conflicts. Like some other railroads, in this infancy of dieselization, the D&RGW wished to adopt a numbering system that might convey more information than mere unit identification. By the time the second order arrived, this time from Baldwin, they had settled on a system based on rated horsepower stated in units of ten.

The new 660 horsepower Baldwin switchers thus were numbered 66-74, the 380 horsepower General Electrics were 38-43 and the NW2 was soon renumbered as 100. The 1000 horsepower switchers subsequently bought from Alco were added to the 100 series as 101-104 and so on. No concern apparently was given to keeping engines of similar power but different builders separate.

In February 1942 the first multiple unit freight power arrived on the property in the form of three 194-foot long, 5400 horsepower EMD locomotives, each consisting of two cab and two booster units. Because they were intended to serve as single pieces of motive power, the numbering system dictated that the road numbers should commence with 540. However, identifying four separate units with the same number displayed in the boards at both ends could soon lead to problems so a suffix was added to a small road number stenciled on the lower rear flank of each carbody. Using the 540 as an example, the cab (A) units carried numbers 540 and 540C with the intermediate booster (B) units marked 540A and 540B. The remainder of that order, 541 & 542 were similarly numbered.

Although widely assumed to be FT models, diesel purists may more accurately label the 540-547 as FS units. According to the "Field Service News" section of a 1947 EMD publication describing the company's models, an FS differs from an FT most noticeably in that it lacks drawbars between the A and B units, having couplers instead. The D&RGW was one of four roads having such units though subsequent locomotives 548-551 had the standard drawbars and were FT's.

A second order followed in 1943 for six sets which tried a different suffix system; identifying the quarters of the whole locomotive by "543 First", "543 Second" etc. The arrival in 1944 of the 548, the first Rio Grande diesel with passenger gearing and steam generators, also marked a further refinement of the numbering. The tacit "¼" term was added resulting in "548 First ¼" on one A unit flank, '548 Second ¼" on the adjoining B unit, and so on.

It should be remembered that early freight hauling diesels were sold on the concept of replacing a less efficient steam engine on a one for one basis with a new locomotive of given size. A 5400 horsepower FT was intended to be the replacement for a 2-8-8-2, for example, on a certain subdivision and was considered a single locomotive. It was some time before railroads took advantage of the building-block flexibility of this new power to routinely match the number of diesel units to the train size. On an occasional basis, however, the train dispatchers began to break up the sets to run power consists of one to three units. The problem which soon arose was that having two trains with the same locomotive number on the road at the same time was an invitation to an accident. The Rio Grande's solution was to add the suffix 'A' to the number boards of one of the cab units whenever a locomotive set was separated. Upon the units return to their original configuration, the letters were removed.

In 1946 another deviation in the system was made with the delivery of three sets of four unit, 6000 horsepower F3's. They should have been the 600 series but because they were more similar in origin, size and tractive effort to the 540-551 series FT's than to the anticipated 6000 horsepower Alcos, they were numbered 552-554. These also received the "¼" subscripts on their flanks. When the duo of classic, three unit, PA-PB-PA locomotives arrived in the Spring of 1947 they assumed numbers 600 and 601. One of these PA units would spend part of its first year as 600A, the single unit power for trains 7 and 8.

1949 saw more deliveries of diesels, this time 6000 horsepower F7's and the flaws in the multiple unit numbering system were becoming more troublesome. It did not make sense to tie up four units in the shop when only one needed servicing. Also, the shippers would be better served if locomotive size was matched to the train rather than waiting for additional carloads to fill out the train to match the locomotive's tonnage rating. As a result, during the first half of 1950 the fleet of covered wagons had a fourth digit added to their road numbers to identify each unit individually. For example, the four unit 548 became 5481, 5482, 5483 and 5484 and the three unit 600 became 6001, 6002 and 6003. The previous nomenclature of "First ¼" or "548A" was eliminated.

In November of that year the first four GP (General Purpose) 7 road switchers were delivered from EMD. Rated at 1500 horsepower each and capable of single unit operation, they could have been numbered in the 150 series. However, the 150-152 Fairbanks-Morse units were markedly different from the GP7's which could be equally at home in the yard or MU-ed on the main line. And because they could be combined into a 6000 horsepower road locomotive they might have also been numbered with the F7's, but since the Rio Grande had recently expanded many of its road numbers to four digits they now had little correlation with unit horsepower. It was decided to leave room in the system for possible future FM switchers or F7's by selecting the horsepower unrelated sequence of 5101-5104 for the newcomers. This signaled the end of the horsepower based numbering scheme.

Five RS-3 model, 1600 horsepower road switchers were delivered in 1951 of Alco class 404-DL-248. Although equipped for multiple unit operation, they were assigned numbers beginning with the even hundreds, in this case 5200-5204. This traditionally indicated independent units, not power intended to be run in sets, but it also showed that the system was having difficulty in determining if a unit was a road or switch engine. The GP7 series was altered to conform to this latest interpretation by renumbering the 5104 as 5100. In 1953, five six-axle SD (Special Duty) 7 locomotives were delivered from EMD. Although of the same manufacture and power as the GP7's, this was a new design intended for drag service and so was given a new number sequence, 5300-5304.

The FT units were modified that same year to allow them to operate with the newer F models at low track speeds. Concrete ballast was added to various places in the carbodies and gear ratios were changed from 62:15 to 65:12 to take advantage of the increased adhesion. The new gearing caused their top speed to be limited, by timetable rule, to 40 mph but also permitted them to run continuously at full power down to 10 mph instead of the previous speed of 14.

The early F units which were intended for passenger service had been purchased with a higher speed 61:16 gear ratio. When it was later determined that the standard freight ratio of 62:15 would also safely permit track speeds of up to 70 mph without traction motor armature damage, that gearing was also adopted as the Grande's passenger standard.

Auxiliary booster unit No. 25 was built in 1953 by the Burnham shop forces from Baldwin switcher No. 68. It was designed to augment the tractive effort of the hump locomotive at the railroad's new East Yard at Grand Junction, Colorado. The Baldwin's engine and most electrical components were removed and a 'slug' of concrete was added for weight. It was equipped with a large antenna to receive signals for the hump locomotive from the yard office. Power for the traction motors was taken from a semi-permanently connected 'master' unit. Fairbanks-Morse switcher 151 was the initial master followed by the 152. When they were retired in early 1966, the duty was assumed by SW1200 No. 130 but this combination proved less successful. The slug was retired as a locomotive on September 15, 1971 after a period of disuse. The traction motors and remaining switchgear were removed and the chassis was used in testing the roads original weigh-in-motion scale at Salt Lake City. Unfortunately, one drawback to her being a former locomotive arose when the couplers, which were mounted rigidly in the vertical plane, were occasionally detected transferring weight to or from adjacent cars when in motion. When a new electronic scale which weighs each freight car one truck at a time was installed at Sake Lake City, No. 25's eight foot truck wheelbase was too long to fit. After some more years of neglect it was retired in 1978.

The Spring of 1955 saw the first purchase of 12 new GP9's. Although essentially a 1750 horsepower upgrade of the GP7, it was determined that these units should be used in four unit sets and so were numbered 5901-5904, 5911-5914 and 5921-5924. Evidently, someone in management still felt that all freight trains came in one size. These GP9's, like the 12 more received in 1956, as well as the F unit fleet, would increasingly be broken up in later years for various assignments. The 5900's were the last attempt to indicate a fixed locomotive consist by the numbering scheme. All diesel units were thereafter numbered into continuous sequences for a given purpose and manufacturer. Horsepower increases or evolutionary changes were not cause for a new sequence. For example, when the SD9 roadswitchers came in 1957 they were added to the SD7 sequence and have since been followed by SD45's and SD40T-2's.

EMD, under pressure from some of its customers for more horsepower, introduced a four axle, turbocharged GP20 in 1959. During tests of the demonstrators on the Rio Grande, it was discovered they would not perform adequately in the frequent tunnels; probably due to the lack of a turbocharger intercooler. At this same time, in Europe, much development work was being done with the diesel-hydraulic locomotive. This design promised better adhesion from its mechanically coupled axles, potentially very important to a mountain railroad, much higher horsepower per unit, and immunity from serious electrical problems. After a period of investigation, the Rio Grande, in a joint venture with the Southern Pacific, contracted for three locomotives each with builder Krauss-Maffei of Munich, Germany. They were each 4000 horsepower, six axle cab units delivered in November 1961. Probably due to their power rating and because they were a design new to the Rio Grande, they received a new number series, 4001-4003.

Many problems were encountered during the time they spent on the D&RGW though the hydraulic transmission was rarely among them. As built, the units had all pneumatic controls which were slow, susceptible to variations in altitude, and prevented MU-ing with diesel-electrics. The controls were soon redesigned by a staff member of the Rio Grande's mechanical department in a major modification that was also adopted by the SP. To allow the engines of trailing units to breath cooler air in tunnels, the air intakes were moved from the slanted part of the roof to just above the frame. A similar remedy would be used by the D&RGW and SP in the 1970's on their EMD SD40/45T-2 'tunnel' locomotives cooling systems. Despite these and many other changes, the company found the KM's to be costing many times more to operate per unit mile than its new GP30's which were proving capable of averaging 16,000 miles a month. The Rio Grande's noble experiment with the diesel-hydraulic ended with the sale of the three ML-4s to the SP in 1964. That road subsequently purchased 18 more such units, three built domestically by Alco, but finally the SP, too, abandoned the type.

At this same time the Grande ventured into the diesel-mechanical locomotive field in a big way with the purchase of a third hand, Davenport 30-ton switcher. This diminutive, narrow gauge ball of fire's primary duties were local Durango switching and wyeing the Silverton train until a balloon track was built for that purpose. She was unceremoniously dropped from the company's Summary of Equipment in 1964 although she was not sold for another six years. Two U.S. Army diesel-electrics were extensively tested on the narrow gauge, a General Electric numbered 3000 and a Davenport-Besler, No. 4700N. In addition, GE and EMD proposed other units over the years but none were ordered.

The 4000's and No. 50 were not the only diesels to fall into disfavor with the Rio Grande's watchful management. The Alco passenger units which were purchased to lead the flagship *California Zephyr* had been gradually displaced to secondary runs by the less troublesome EMD F's. The two PB units had their engines and electrical gear removed in 1965 and the carbodies rebuilt into steam generator cars using boilers left over from traded-in F units. Because their larger water capacity permits greater range between refill points than the F9's, these cars supplement the *Rio Grande Zephyr* consist during cold months.

There are two other steam generator cars left in 1980, Nos. 250 and 251, both converted from steam locomotive tenders. Car 250 is assigned to Salt Lake City as emergency protection for RGZ service and 251 runs each winter on the GP40 powered, Winter Park ski trains.

The Rio Grande bought its first generation of diesels from each of the major builders except Lima. This allowed the company to evaluate the merits of each manufacturer in an era when the design of diesel locomotives was open to a variety of interpretations. After that first decade however, the D&RGW has maintained a monogamous relationship with EMD from which it has rarely strayed. The units from LaGrange were found to be more reliable and cheaper to maintain, especially the diesel powerplant, than most of the competition. Also, by buying from one builder with a highly standardized product line, the shop forces were required to learn only EMD's maintenance and troubleshooting procedures and to stock only one line of replacement parts. On a modestly sized railroad, that resulted in significant savings.

The railroad's present locomotive (other than steam) class designation contains three pieces of information:

1. Power source and transmission
2. Wheel arrangement using AAR code
3. Nominal maximum tractive effort expressed in thousands of pounds

Tractive effort, the pulling force at the coupler, is a wide ranging variable that is subject to a number of functions but for simplicity, starting (or maximum) tractive effort may be approximated by multiplying the locomotive weight on its driving wheels times a factor of adhesion. Early Rio Grande classes of switch engines used a 30% adhesion factor multiplied by the total loaded weight to arrive at their nominal maximum T.E.

The 230,000-pound Alco S-2's, for example, were classed DE B−B 69. When the multiple unit FT's 540-547 were delivered, they were classed DE B−B+B−B+B−B+B−B 226. This T.E. figure was arrived at by using a more reasonable 25% factor of adhesion multiplied by the weight of the four units carrying one half of their variable supplies (fuel, sand and boiler water). This lengthy wheel arrangement code for multiple unit locomotives was cumbersome, so after World War II those classes were simplified, in this case to DE 4 B−B 226. In 1961, all of the multiple units were reclassified as individual units, reflecting the fact they were no longer being operated in their original sets. Thus the 5401, by then regeared and ballasted, became a DE B−B 60. This system remains in effect in 1980 with T.E. being derived by using 25% adhesion with one half variable supplies.

ROSTER EXPLANATIONS

1. Weight and tractive effort figures shown are averages for each locomotive group.
2. Data in the roster refers to the locomotive in its final form before leaving the D&RGW or is current to 1980 for units presently owned.
3. Dates in the disposition column are normally the date the unit left the property rather than the date of sale or trade-in agreement.
4. Tractive efforts for road units, road switchers and second generation yard switchers are calculated using unit weight with one half variable supplies at 25% adhesion. First generation switchers except No. 100 and booster No. 25 were figured using the units total loaded weight at 30% adhesion.
5. Weights given are the total loaded weight.

Notes — Additions — Corrections

D&RGW Motive Power — 1983

ROAD NOS.	UNITS	LOCO TYPE	BUILT	BUILDER	CLASS	WEIGHT Tons	LENGTH Ft-In	TRACTION Hp	ENGINE TYPE	GEN/ALT TYPE	BRAKE EQUIP.	COOLANT Gal	FUEL Gal	LUBE OIL Gal
130-139	10	SW1200	1965	EMD	DE B-B 61	123	44-5	1200	12-567C	D25C	26-L	230	930	165
140-146	7	SW1000	1966	"	DE B-B 60	123	44-8	1000	8-645E	D25C	26-L	190	1100	135
147-149	3	SW1000	1968	"	DE B-B 60	123	44-8	1000	8-645E	D25C	26-L	190	1100	135
3001-3013	10	GP30	1962	"	DE B-B 62	129	56-2	2250	16-567D3	D22DT	26-L	227	2600	220
3014-3028	15 #	GP30	1963	"	DE B-B 62	130	56-2	2250	16-567D3	D22DT	26-L	227	2600	220
3029-3038	10	GP35	1964	"	DE B-B 62	130	56-2	2500	16-567D3A	D32	26-L	275	2600	243
3039-3050	12	GP35	1965	"	DE B-B 62	130	56-2	2500	16-567D3A	D32	26-L	275	2600	243
3051-3068	17 #	GP40	1966	"	DE B-B 65	138	59-2	3000	16-645E3	AR10	26-L	254	3600	396
3069-3080	12	GP40	1967	"	DE B-B 65	138	59-2	3000	16-645E3	AR10	26-L	254	3600	396
3081-3085	5	GP40	1969	"	DE B-B 65	138	59-2	3000	16-645E3	AR10	26-L	254	3600	396
3086-3093	8	GP40	1971	"	DE B-B 65	138	59-2	3000	16-645E3	AR10	26-L	254	3600	396
3094-3105	12	GP40-2	1972	"	DE B-B 65	139	59-2	3000	16-645E3	AR10	26-L	275	3600	396
3106-3115	10	GP40-2	1973	"	DE B-B 65	139	59-2	3000	16-645E3	AR10	26-L	275	3600	396
3116-3128	13	GP40-2	1974	"	DE B-B 65	139	59-2	3000	16-645E3	AR10 *	26-L	275	3600	396
3129-3130	2	GP40-2	Note 4	"	DE B-B 67	141	59-2	3000	16-645E3C	AR10 *	26-L	275	3600	396
5108	1	GP7	1952	"	DE B-B 60	122	55-11	1500	16-567B	D12B	24-RL	230	1200	200
5300-5304	5	SD7	1953	"	DE C-C 89	184	60-8½	1500	16-567B	D12C	24-RL	260	2400	200
5305-5314	10	SD9	1957	"	DE C-C 89	184	60-8½	1750	16-567C	D12C	24-RL	260	2400	200
5315-5324	10	SD45	1967	"	DE C-C 93	195	65-9½	3600	20-645E3	AR10	26-L	288	4000	466
5325-5340	16	SD45	1968	"	DE C-C 93	195	65-9½	3600	20-645E3	AR10	26-L	288	4000	466
5341-5355	15	SD40T-2	1974	"	DE C-C 92	194	70-8	3000	16-645E3	AR10 *	26-L	275	4000	396
5356-5373	18	SD40T-2	1975	"	DE C-C 92	194	70-8	3000	16-645E3	AR10 *	26-L	275	4000	396
5374-5385	12	SD40T-2	1977	"	DE C-C 92	194	70-8	3000	16-645E3	AR10 *	26-L	275	4000	396
5386-5397	12	SD40T-2	1978	"	DE C-C 92	194	70-8	3000	16-645E3	AR10 *	26-L	275	4000	396
5398-5413	16	SD40T-2	1980	"	DE C-C 92	194	70-8	3000	16-645E3B	AR10 *	26-L	275	4000	396
5762-5763	2	F9B	1955	"	DE B-B 59	124	50-0	1750	16-567C	D12 *	24-RL	215	1200	200
5771	1	F9A	1955	"	DE B-B 60	124	50-8	1750	16-567C	D12 *	24-RL	230	1200	200
5902-5904	3	GP9	1955	"	DE B-B 60	123	56-2	1750	16-567C	D12B	24-RL	230	1200	200
5911-5914	4	GP9	1955	"	DE B-B 60	123	56-2	1750	16-567C	D12B	24-RL	230	1200	200
5921-5924	3	GP9	1955	"	DE B-B 60	123	56-2	1750	16-567C	D12B	24-RL	230	1200	200
5931-5934	3	GP9	1956	"	DE B-B 61	125	56-2	1750	16-567C	D12B	24-RL	230	1600	200
5941-5944	3	GP9	1956	"	DE B-B 61	125	56-2	1750	16-567C	D12B	24-RL	230	1600	200
5951-5954	4	GP9	1956	"	DE B-B 61	125	56-2	1750	16-567C	D12B	24-RL	230	1600	200

TOTAL UNITS 282 as of 1-1-83

Office of the Chief Mechanical Officer 1/1/1983

ROAD NOS.		UNITS	BOILERS / Unit	BUILT CARBODY	BUILT as S.G.	BUILDER	BOILER WATER Gal	FUEL OIL Gal	LOADED WT Lbs	STEAM CAPY Lbs/Hr
250	Steam Generator Car	1	2	1938	1953	Baldwin;D&RGW	8200	1200	251,600	5500
251	"	1	2	1938	1953	Baldwin;D&RGW	8200	1200	251,600	6500
252,253	"	2	2	1947	1965	Alco;D&RGW	6730	1200	244,680**	6500
5762,5763	Loco Units with Steam Generators	2	1	1955	1955	EMD	1400	1200	247,390	3250
5771	Loco Unit with Water Tank only	1	0	1955	1955	EMD	600	1200	247,706	0

* 18 Kw Aux generator

Note 1. Length is over coupler pulling faces; free.

2. All units have 40" dia. wheels except 250,251 (36" dia.)

3. Weights include full load of variable supplies.

4. Scheduled delivery during year.

DIESEL ENGINE TYPE

16-	Number of cylinders
645	Cu.In. displacement/cyl.
E3	Model

** Unit 253 weight is 193,000 lbs.

One unit scheduled for retirement.

CLASS DESIGNATION

DE	Diesel Electric	B-B	2 driving axles/truck	00	Starting tractive effort in 1000 lbs. @25% adh.½ var.supply
		C-C	3 driving axles/truck		

AUXILIARY BOOSTER (SLUG)

B-B BLW/D&RGW No Class 76:16 241,000# 47,200# TE

25 #62502-7/41 Conv. 6/53 from V0660 68; Conv. to Scale Test Car 25, 8/72; Sold through Luria Bros., Inc. to Intermountain Steel & Supply Co., Salt Lake City, 6/13/78.

44-TON 380 hp

B-B GE DE B-B 26 $11^1/_4$:1 89,000# 26,400# TE

38 #13096-8/41 Sold 12/3/64 to Manufacturers Equipment Co., Cleveland, Ohio; Resold to Great Lakes Carbon Co. 12, St. Louis, Mo.

39 #15123-9/42 Sold 6/28/49 to Sanford & Eastern RR 1st 14; Resold 1960 to Hoosac Tunnel & Wilmington 16.

40 #15127-9/42 Sold 5/14/54 to Great Western Sugar Co. 40, Johnstown, Colo.

41 #15128-9/42 Sold 8/5/54 to Utah Power & Light Co. 41, Castle Gate, Utah.

42 #15129-9/42 Sold for scrap 11/18/64 to Barter Machinery & Supply Co., Denver.

43 #15130-9/42 Sold 6/28/49 to Sanford & Eastern RR 15; Resold 7/49 to Hoosac Tunnel & Wilmington 15; Resold 11/56 to Claremont & Concord 15; Resold to Raymond International 4402.

Note: A further unit, to have been numbered 44, was diverted to the U.S. Navy.

30-TON DIESEL MECHANICAL 200hp NARROW GAUGE

50 *See page 27.*

VO 660 660 hp

B-B Baldwin DE B-B 60 68:14 198,500# 59,700# TE

66 #62496-5/41 Traded in to EMD 1/23/67 on SD45.

67 #62501-7/41 Sold for scrap 4/66 to Barter Machinery & Supply Co., Denver.

68 #62502-7/41 Conv. 6/53 to Auxiliary Booster 25.

69 #64183-8/41 Sold for scrap 4/66 to Barter Machinery & Supply Co., Denver.

70 #64184-8/41 Traded in to EMD 1/23/67 on SD45.

71 #64185-8/41 Sold for scrap 11/5/64 to Barter Machinery & Supply Co., Denver.

72 #64186-8/41 Traded in to EMD 1/23/67 on SD45.

73 #64187-8/41 Traded in to EMD 1/23/67 on SD45.

74 #64188-8/41 Traded in to EMD 1/23/67 on SD45.

NW2 1000 hp

B-B EMC DE B-B 61 62:15 248,880# 61,390# TE

100 #1313-1/41 *Reno from 7000, 9/13/41. Equipped with trolley pole to activate signals on Denver & Intermountain until 7/53. Sold 1/19/68 to Precision Engineering Co., Mt. Vernon, Ill.; Resold to Great Lakes Steel Corp., Detroit, Mich. Resold to East Camden & Highland RR in Arkansas, 1972, Rblt to SW1200 specifications and renumbered 60.*

Scale test car 25 at Salt Lake City in 1972 had started life as Baldwin V0660 switcher 68 before being converted to auxiliary booster 25 for service on the hump at East Yard, Grand Junction. (Ed Fulcomer)

No. 38 was the last of the six 44-ton GE units to survive on the roster. It is shown outside the diesel shop at Burnham in the summer of 1964. (Ed Fulcomer)

Baldwin No. 73, the next-to-the-last of the long line of locomotives purchased by the D&RGW from this famous builder over a seventy year span, idles in the Alamosa yard in October 1966. Note the dual gauge coupler; Alco's 110-111 had also been equipped with these at one time. (Ed Fulcomer)

No. 7000 works Pueblo Union Depot less than a month after its delivery in early 1941 (Richard H. Kindig–Ed Fulcomer Collection). Soon renumbered 100, it was still sub-numbered 7000 when the photo below right was taken. It also had received extended exhaust stacks and a cab bay window. (Michael Davis Collection)

S2 1000 hp

B-B ALCO DE B-B 69 75:16 230,000# 69,000# TE

101	#69555-9/41	Sold for scrap 4/8/66 to Precision Engineering Co., Mt. Vernon, Ill.
102	#69557-9/41	Sold for scrap 7/23/65 to Barter Machinery & Supply Co., Denver.
103	#69558-9/41	Sold for scrap 11/5/64 to Barter Machinery & Supply Co., Denver.
104	#69559-9/41	Sold for scrap 8/27/64 to Barter Machinery & Supply Co., Denver.
105	#70074-3/43	Sold for scrap 4/8/66 to Precision Engineering Co., Mt. Vernon, Ill.
106	#70075-3/43	Sold for scrap 7/23/65 to Barter Machinery & Supply Co., Denver.
107	#70076-5/43	Sold for scrap 10/24/64 to Barter Machinery & Supply Co., Denver.
108	#70077-5/43	Sold 3/3/64 to Preston W. Duffy & Co., Columbus, Ohio; Resold to Wierton Steel Corp., Wierton, W. Va. 215.
109	#70183-9/43	Sold 2/5/65 to Luria Bros., Inc., Pueblo, Colo.; Resold to Colorado & Wyoming RR 1105, Minnequa, Colo.
110	#70184-9/43	Sold 8/14/63 to George R. Silcott, Worthington, Ohio; Resold 8/63 to Kentucky & Tennessee RR 101.
111	#70185-9/43	Sold for scrap 4/8/66 to Precision Engineering Co., Mt. Vernon, Ill.; subsequently traded 12/66 to George R. Silcott, Worthington, Ohio, who then leased the unit to Republic Steel Corp.
112	#70186-9/43	Sold for scrap 7/23/65 to Barter Machinery & Supply Co., Denver.
113	#70187-9/43	Sold for scrap 11/3/64 to Barter Machinery & Supply Co., Denver.
114	#70188-9/43	Sold 5/26/65 to William W. Taggart, Dallas, Tex.; Resold 7/65 to Gifford-Hill & Co., Texarkana, Tex.
115	#70195-3/44	Sold 10/3/64 to United Electric Coal Co. 115, Canton, Ill.
116	#70196-3/44	Sold 6/9/65 to Luria Bros., Inc., Pueblo, Colo.; Resold to Colorado & Wyoming RR 1104 Minnequa, Colo.
117	#72050-5/44	Sold 6/3/65 to William W. Taggart, Dallas, Tex.; Resold 7/65 to Goodpasture Grain & Milling Co. 117, Galena Park (Houston), Tex.
118	#72051-5/44	Sold 8/14/63 to George R. Silcott, Worthington, Ohio; Resold 8/63 to Kentucky & Tennessee RR 102.
119	#72052-5/44	Sold 8/14/63 to George R. Silcott, Worthington, Ohio; Re-sold 8/63 to Kentucky & Tennessee RR 103.

H10-44 1000 hp

B-B Fairbanks-Morse DE B-B 72 68:14 240,955# 72,286# TE

120	#10L53-4/48	Traded in to EMD 1/23/67 SD45.
121	#10L54-4/48	Traded to EMD 1/23/67 on SD45.
122	#10L55-4/48	Sold for scrap 1/19/68 to Precision Engineering Co., Mt. Vernon, Ill.; Resold to SLSF RR 286.
123	#10L58-4/48	Sold for scrap 1/29/68 to Precision Engineering Co., Mt. Vernon, Ill.

SW1200 1200 hp

B-B EMD DE B-B 61 62:15 246,460# 60,544# TE

130 #30016-12/64 Equipped to mate with Auxiliary Booster 25 at Grand Junction until 8/72.

131 #30017-12/64

132 #30018-1/65

133 #30019-1/65

134 #30020-1/65

135 #30024-1/65

136 #30025-1/65

137 #30026-1/65

138 #30027-1/65

139 #30028-1/65

SW1000 1000 hp

B-B EMD DE B-B 61 62:15 246,783# (140-146) 60,377# TE

247,403# (147-149) 60,480# TE

140 #32175-9/66

141 #32176-9/66

142 #32177-9/66

143 #32178-10/66

144 #32179-10/66

145 #32180-10/66

146 #32313-10/66

147 #33915-4/68

148 #33916-4/68

149 #33917-4/68

Note: Units 147-149 have roller bearing trucks, while units 140-146 have friction bearing trucks.

H15-44 1500 hp

B-B Fairbanks-Morse DE B-B 72 63:15 240,900# 72,270# TE

150 #15L03-1/48 Sold for scrap 4/8/66 to Precision Engineering Co., Mt. Vernon, Ill.

151 #15L04-2/48 Sold for scrap 4/8/66 to Precision Engineering Co., Mt. Vernon, Ill.

152 #15L05-2/48 Sold for scrap 4/8/66 to Precision Engineering Co., Mt. Vernon, Ill.

Note: Units 151 and 152 were equipped for use with Auxiliary Booster 25 at Grand Junction.

GP30 2250 hp

B-B EMD DE B-B 62 62:15 257,508# (3001-13) 61,773# TE

260,660# (3014-28) 62,088# TE

3001 #27135-4/62

3002 #27136-4/62 Damaged, Swan, Colo., 9/22/70; Reblt by EMD.

3003 #27137-4/62 Damaged, Crater, Colo., 12/25/68; Reblt by EMD.

3004 #27138-4/62

3005 #27139-4/62 Destroyed, Swan, Colo., 9/22/70; Ret 12/70.

3006 #27140-4/62

3007	#27141-4/62	
3008	#27142-5/62	
3009	#27143-5/62	Destroyed, Brendel, Utah, 9/21/74; Ret 1/75. Salvage traded in to EMD; Frame sold to Barter Machinery & Supply Co., Denver, 11/25/74.
3010	#27144-5/62	
3011	#27222-5/62	
3012	#27223-5/62	Destroyed, Cedarwood, Colo., 6/10/71; Ret 1/72.
3013	#27224-5/62	
3014	#28043-1/63	Damaged, Crater, Colo., 12/25/68; Reblt by EMD.
3015	#28044-2/63	
3016	#28045-2/63	
3017	#28046-2/63	
3018	#28047-2/63	
3019	#28048-2/63	
3020	#28049-2/63	Leased to Kennecott Copper Corp. 704, Returned 3/77.
3021	#28050-2/63	Leased to Kennecott Copper Corp. 722, Returned 2/79.
3022	#28051-2/63	Leased to Kennecott Copper Corp. 726, Returned 2/79.
3023	#28052-2/63	Damaged, Swan, Colo., 9/22/70; Reblt by EMD.
3024	#28053-2/63	
3025	#28054-2/63	Destroyed at Byers Canyon 8/7/82.
3026	#28055-2/63	
3027	#28056-2/63	Damaged, Crater, Colo., 12/25/68; Reblt by EMD. Leased to Kennecott Copper Corp. 701, Returned 3/77.
3028	#28057-2/63	

Note: Units 3021-3028 were modified as B-units in 1972 and are no longer used as control units on the point of trains.
Note: Units were leased to Kennecott Copper Corp. for a period of approximately two years.

GP35 2500 hp

B-B	*EMD*	*DE B-B 62*	*62:15*	*260,482# (3029-38)*	*62,254# TE*
				259,789# (3039-50)	*61,944# TE*

3029	#29260-5/64	
3030	#29261-5/64	
3031	#29262-5/64	
3032	#29263-5/64	
3033	#29264-5/64	
3034	#29265-6/64	
3035	#29266-6/64	
3036	#29267-6/64	
3037	#29370-6/64	
3038	#29371-6/64	
3039	#29964-12/64	
3040	#29965-12/64	
3041	#29966-12/64	
3042	#29967-12/64	
3043	#29968-12/64	
3044	#29969-12/64	
3045	#29970-12/64	
3046	#29971-12/64	
3047	#29972-12/64	
3048	#29973-1/65	Damaged, Swan, Colo., 9/22/70; Reblt by EMD.
3049	#29974-1/65	
3050	#30023-1/65	

Note: Units 3029-3050 were modified as B-units in 1972 and are no longer used as control units on the point of trains.

(top) *Alco No. 114, badly in need of paint, awaits sale at Burnham in 1965.* (Ed Fulcomer) *Fairbanks-Morse No. 121, at Denver Union Station, December 27, 1966, would be gone from the roster the following month.* (F. Hol Wagner, Jr.)

Replacements for the Grande's motley assortment of first generation switchers were SW1200's and SW1000's from EMD, as seen below at Colorado Springs and North Yard, Denver. (Thomas P. Lyons)

Massive No. 150 from Fairbanks-Morse looked quite capable of moving coal over Soldier Summit when its portrait was made by Otto Perry at Helper, Utah, on Independence Day, 1949. (Denver Public Library, Western History Collection)

There is no mistaking No. 3016, shown at Pueblo in 1973, as being a GP30, but only a diesel fan could easily distinguish GP35 No. 3046, emerging from Tunnel No. 1 on the Moffat Route, from a GP40 such as 3075 below. (right top and bottom, Bruce D. Barrett)

GP40 3000 hp

B-B	*EMD*	*DE B-B 65*	*62:15*	*276,545# (3051-3062)*	*65,195# TE*
				278-050# (3063)	*65,571# TE*
				275,856# (3064-3068)	*64,980# TE*
				276,352# (3069-3080)	*65,072# TE*
				277,180# (3081-3085)	*65,234# TE*
				276,617# (3086-3093)	*65,093# TE*

3051	#30995-1/66	
3052	#30996-1/66	
3053	#30997-1/66	
3054	#30998-1/66	
3055	#30999-1/66	
3056	#31000-1/66	
3057	#31001-1/66	
3058	#31002-1/66	Destroyed at Byers Canyon 8/7/82.
3059	#31003-1/66	
3060	#31004-1/66	
3061	#31005-1/66	
3062	#31006-1/66	
3063	#31440-1/66	Destroyed, Hideaway Park, Colo., 6/5/74; Ret 12/3/74. Traded in on #3128.
3064	#32170-9/66	
3065	#32171-9/66	
3066	#32172-9/66	
3067	#32173-9/66	
3068	#32174-9/66	
3069	#32880-2/67	
3070	#32881-2/67	
3071	#32882-2/67	
3072	#32883-2/67	
3073	#32884-2/67	
3074	#32885-2/67	
3075	#32886-2/67	Electrical fire 8/17/82. Rblt as GP40-2.
3076	#32887-2/67	
3077	#32888-2/67	
3078	#32889-2/67	
3079	#32890-2/67	
3080	#32891-2/67	
3081	#35577-10/69	Wrecked 9/1/72, rebuilt as GP40-2.
3082	#35578-10/69	
3083	#35579-10/69	
3084	#35580-10/69	
3085	#35581-10/69	
3086	#38571-11/71	
3087	#38572-11/71	
3088	#38573-11/71	
3089	#38574-11/71	
3090	#38575-11/71	
3091	#38576-11/71	
3092	#38577-11/71	
3093	#38578-11/71	

Note: Units 3051-3075 were modified as B-units in 1972 and are no longer used as control units on the point of trains.

GP40-2 3000 hp

B-B	*EMD*	*DE B-B 65*	*62:15*	*277,348# (3094-3105)*	*65,298# TE*
				276,933# (3106-3115)	*65,171# TE*
				277,343# (3116-3128)	*65,242# TE*

3094	#7360-1—4/72	
3095	#7360-2—4/72	
3096	#7360-3—4/72	
3097	#7360-4—4/72	
3098	#7360-5—4/72	
3099	#7360-6—4/72	
3100	#7360-7—4/72	
3101	#7360-8—4/72	
3102	#7360-9—4/72	
3103	#7360-10—4/72	
3104	#7360-11—4/72	
3105	#7360-12—4/72	
3106	#72715-1—12/72	
3107	#72715-2—12/72	
3108	#72715-3—12/72	
3109	#72715-4—12/72	
3110	#72715-5—12/72	
3111	#72715-6—12/72	
3112	#72715-7—12/72	
3113	#72715-8—12/72	
3114	#72715-9—12/72	
3115	#72715-10—12/72	
3116	#74635-1—9/74	
3117	#74635-2—9/74	
3118	#74635-3—9/74	
3119	#74635-4—9/74	
3120	#74635-5—9/74	
3121	#74635-6—9/74	
3122	#74635-7—9/74	
3123	#74635-8—9/74	
3124	#74635-9—9/74	
3125	#74635-10—9/74	
3126	#74635-11—9/74	
3127	#74635-12—9/74	
3128	#74735-1—11/74	Built to replace 3063.
3129	#827038-1— /83	
3130	#827038-2— /83	

ML-4 4000 hp

C-C	*Krauss-Maffei*	*DH C-C 104*	*330,327#*	*104,080# TE*

4001	#18697-6/61	Sold 2/6/64 to Southern Pacific 9021; Reno 9103, 11/65. Ret 12/31/67 and scrapped.
4002	#18698-6/61	Sold 2/6/64 to Southern Pacific 9022; Reno 9104, 11/65. Ret 12/31/67 and scrapped.
4003	#18699-6/61	Sold 2/6/64 to Southern Pacific 9023; Reno 9105, 11/65. Ret 12/31/67 and scrapped.

GP7 1500 hp

B-B	*EMD*	*DE B-B 60*	*62:15*	*245,960# (5100-5103)*	*60,198# TE*
				244,834# (5104-5113)	*59,919# TE*

5100	#11428-10/50	Reno from 5104(1st), 11/28/51. Traded in to EMD 3/2/72 on GP40-2.
5101	#11425-10/50	Sold 11/6/72 to Rock Island 4200; Reblt and reno 4485, then 4473.
5102	#11426-10/50	Sold 10/28/72 to Rock Island 4201; Resold 5/77 to Precision National Corp., Mt. Vernon, Ill.
5103	#11427-10/50	Sold 10/28/72 to Rock Island 4202; Resold 5/77 to Precision National Corp., Mt. Vernon, Ill.
5104 (1st)	#11428-10/50	Reno 5100, 11/28/51.
5104 (2nd)	#14429-6/52	Traded in to EMD 3/2/72 on GP40-2.
5105	#14430-6/52	Sold 11/12/72 to Rock Island 4203; Reblt and reno 4488, then 4474.
5106	#14431-6/52	Sold 11/8/72 to Rock Island 4204; Resold 5/77 to Precision National Corp., Mt. Vernon, Ill.
5107	#14432-6/52	Sold 11/16/72 to Rock Island 4205; Reblt and reno 4441.
5108	#14433-6/52	In service, 1983.
5109	#16543-6/52	Traded in to EMD 1/26/72 on GP40-2.
5110	#16544-6/52	Sold 11/8/72 to Rock Island 4206; Resold 5/77 to Precision National Corp., Mt. Vernon, Ill.
5111	#16545-6/52	Sold 11/26/72 to Rock Island 4207; Resold 5/77 to Precision National Corp., Mt. Vernon, Ill.
5112	#16546-6/52	Sold 10/26/72 to Rock Island 4208; Reblt and reno 4442.
5113	#16547-6/52	Sold 11/3/72 to Rock Island 4209; Reblt and reno 4443.

RS3 1600 hp

B-B	*ALCO*	*DE B-B 60*	*74:18*	*248,000#*	*60,198# TE*

5200	#78895-6/51	Sold for scrap 4/8/66 to Precision Engineering Co., Mt. Vernon, Ill.
5201	#78896-6/51	Sold for scrap 4/8/66 to Precision Engineering Co., Mt. Vernon, Ill.
5202	#78897-6/51	Sold for scrap 4/8/66 to Precision Engineering Co., Mt. Vernon, Ill.
5203	#78898-6/51	Sold for scrap 4/8/66 to Precision Engineering Co., Mt. Vernon, Ill.
5204	#78899-6/51	Sold for scrap 4/8/66 to Precision Engineering Co., Mt. Vernon, Ill.

SD7 1500 hp

C-C EMD DE C-C 89 62:15 368,300# 89,294# TE

5300 #18124-5/53

5301 #18125-5/53

5302 #18126-5/53

5303 #18127-5/53

5304 #18128-5/53

SD9 1750 hp

C-C EMD DE C-C 89 62:15 367,020# 89,844# TE

5305 #22808-7/57 Damaged, Pueblo, Colo., 4/26/72; Reblt by D&RGW 9/72 with chopnose and assigned as hump engine, East Yard, Grand Junction, Colo.

5306 #22809-7/57

5307 #22810-7/57

5308 #22811-7/57

5309 #22812-7/57

5310 #22813-7/57

5311 #22814-7/57

5312 #22815-7/57

5313 #22816-7/57

5314 #22817-7/57

SD45 3600 hp

C-C EMD DE C-C 93 62:15 389,380# (5315-5324) 92,980# TE
389,294# (5325-5340) 92,909# TE

5315 #32689-1/67

5316 #32690-1/67

5317 #32691-1/67

5318 #32692-1/67

5319 #32693-1/67

5320 #32694-1/67

5321 #32695-1/67

5322 #32696-1/67

5323 #32697-1/67

5324 #32698-2/67

5325 #33757-3/68

5326 #33758-3/68

5327 #33759-3/68

5328 #33760-3/68

5329 #33761-4/68 Damaged, Crater, Colo., 12/25/68; Reblt by EMD.

5330 #33762-4/68

5331 #33763-4/68

5332 #33764-4/68

5333 #33765-5/68 Damaged, Crater, Colo., 12/25/68; Reblt by EMD.

5334 #33766-4/68

5335 #33767-5/68

5336 #33768-4/68

5337 #33931-3/68

5338 #33932-3/68

5339 #33933-3/68

5340 #33934-3/68

Note: Units 5326-5328 and 5336-5338 were modified for unit coal train service between Sunnyside, Utah and Fontana, Calif. They were pooled on these coal trains with Union Pacific SD45's. Units 5337-5338 were removed from this service in August 1980. All remaining units have since been returned to the Rio Grande.

Just delivered from La Grange in December 1972 GP40-2 3108 sparkles in the afternoon sun at North Yard, Denver. The restyled flying "Rio Grande" is quite distinctive. Rio Grande road power, unlike that of competitor Union Pacific, is seldom seen in such immaculate condition. (Ronald C. Hill)

In spite of their rugged appearance, the German-built hydraulics soon proved to be unsuccessful. The 4002 is at Burnham in June 1962. (F. Hol Wagner, Jr.)

Seventeen year old GP7 5106 is spotted under the Grande's neon sign aimed at motorists on West 6th Avenue in Denver. (F. Hol Wagner, Jr.)RS3 5204 at North Yard was brand new when this photo was taken and illustrates the original road switcher paint scheme. Large numbers were later added below the cab windows and at each end. (Ross Grenard)

SD40T-2   3000 hp

C-C	*EMD*	*DE C-C 92*	*62:15*	*387,022#* *(5341-5355)*	*92,331# TE*
				387,115# *(5356-5373)*	*92,188# TE*
				386,628# *(5374-5385)*	*92,063# TE*
				390,842# *(5386-5397)*	*93,116# TE*
				389,464# *(5398-5413)*	*92,772# TE*

5341 #74636-1—10/74
5342 #74636-2—10/74
5343 #74636-3—10/74
5344 #74636-4—10/74
5345 #74636-5—10/74
5346 #74636-6—10/74
5347 #74636-7—10/74
5348 #74636-8—10/74
5349 #74636-9—10/74
5350 #74636-10—10/74
5351 #74636-11—10/74
5352 #74636-12—10/74
5353 #74636-13—10/74
5354 #74636-14—10/74
5355 #74636-15—10/74
5356 #756046-1—7/75
5357 #756046-2—7/75
5358 #756046-3—7/75
5359 #756046-4—7/75
5360 #756046-5—7/75
5361 #756046-6—7/75
5362 #756046-7—7/75
5363 #756046-8—7/75
5364 #756046-9—8/75
5365 #756046-10—7/75
5366 #756046-11—7/75
5367 #756046-12—8/75
5368 #756046-13—8/75
5369 #756046-14—8/75
5370 #756046-15—8/75
5371 #756046-16—8/75
5372 #756046-17—8/75
5373 #756046-18—8/75
5374 #766050-1—1/77
5375 #766050-2—1/77
5376 #766050-3—1/77
5377 #766050-4—1/77
5378 #766050-5—1/77
5379 #766050-6—1/77
5380 #766050-7—1/77
5381 #766050-8—1/77
5382 #766050-9—1/77
5383 #766050-10—1/77
5384 #766050-11—1/77
5385 #766050-12—1/77
5386 #776098-1—8/78
5387 #776098-2—8/78
5388 #776098-3—8/78
5389 #776098-4—8/78
5390 #776098-5—8/78
5391 #776098-6—8/78
5392 #776098-7—8/78
5393 #776098-8—8/78
5394 #776098-9—8/78
5395 #776098-10—8/78
5396 #776098-11—8/78
5397 #776098-12—8/78
5398 #786264-1—3/30
5399 #786264-2—3/80
5400 #786264-3—3/80
5401 #786264-4—3/80
5402 #786264-5—3/80
5403 #786264-6—3/80
5404 #786264-7—3/80
5405 #786264-8—3/80
5406 #786264-9—3/80
5407 #786264-10—3/80
5408 #786264-11—3/80
5409 #786264-12—3/80
5410 #786264-13—3/80
5411 #786264-14—3/80
5412 #786264-15—3/80
5413 #786264-16—3/80

The D&RGW's first SD7 demonstrates the massive underframe and indented classification lights that identify these EMD units. SD9 No. 5305 was rebuilt with a low nose. Both were photographed at Pueblo in 1972. (Bruce D. Barrett)

The size of SD45 5340 is emphasized by comparison with the GP35 behind it. (Bruce D. Barrett) Tunnel motors 5380 and 5344 lead an empty coal train at Coal Creek, Colorado, in May 1977. Only Rio Grande and Southern Pacific have these units with low mounted air intakes and oversize radiators designed to cope with miles of tunnels and snowsheds. (Ronald C. Hill)

FT 5400 hp (1350 hp per unit)

B-B	*EMD*	*DE B-B 60 (5401-5474)*	*65:12*[1]	*977,250#*[1]	*238,980# TE*[1]
		DE B-B 57 (5481-5484)	*61:16*	*945,960#*	*228,380# TE*
		DE B-B 60 (5491-5514)	*65:12*[1]	*977,250#*[1]	*239,010# TE*[1]

5401 #1435-1/42 A Reno from 540, 2/8/50. Traded in to EMD 4/24/64 on GP35.

5402 #1441-1/42 B Reno from 540, 2/8/50. Traded in to EMD 4/24/64 on GP35.

5403 #1442-1/42 B Reno from 540, 2/8/50. Traded in to EMD 12/26/62 on GP30.

5404 #1436-1/42 A Reno from 540, 2/8/50. Traded in to EMD 2/28/64 on GP30.

5411 #1437-1/42 A Reno from 541, 1/25/50. Traded in to EMD 12/23/64 on GP35.

5412 #1443-1/42 B Reno from 541, 1/25/50. Traded in to EMD 12/26/62 on GP30.

5413 #1444-1/42 B Reno from 541, 1/25/50. Traded in to EMD 12/26/62 on GP30.

5414 #1438-1/42 A Reno from 541, 1/25/50. Traded in to EMD 3/1/62 on GP30.

5421 #1439-2/42 A Reno from 542, 2/27/50. Traded in to EMD 1/11/65 on GP35.

5422 #1445-2/42 B Reno from 542, 2/27/50. Traded in to EMD 1/11/65 on GP35.

5423 #1446-2/42 B Reno from 542, 2/27/50. Traded in to EMD 2/22/62 on GP30.

5424 #1440-2/42 A Reno from 542, 2/27/50. Traded in to EMD 4/24/64 on GP35.

5431 #1892-5/43 A Reno from 543, 1/31/50. Traded in to EMD 2/28/62 on GP30.

5432 #1904-5/43 B Reno from 543, 1/31/50. Traded in to EMD 4/4/62 on GP30.

5433 #1905-5/43 B Reno from 543, 1/31/50. Traded in to EMD 3/10/64 on GP35.

5434 #1893-5/43 A Reno from 543, 1/31/50. Traded in to EMD 1/11/65 on GP35.

5441 #1894-5/43 A Reno from 544, 3/17/50. Traded in to EMD 12/23/64 on GP35.

5442 #1906-5/43 B Reno from 544, 3/17/50. Traded in to EMD 2/62 on GP30.

5443 #1907-5/43 B Reno from 544, 3/17/50. Traded in to EMD 12/23/64 on GP35.

5444 #1895-5/43 A Reno from 544, 3/17/50. Traded in to EMD 12/3/62 on GP30.

5451 #1896-6/43 A Reno from 545, 4/6/50. Traded in to EMD 12/26/62 on GP30.

5452 #1908-6/43 B Reno from 545, 4/6/50. Traded in to EMD 12/23/64 on GP35.

5453 #1909-6/43 B Reno from 545, 4/6/50. Traded in to EMD 12/20/62 on GP30.

5454 #1897-6/43 A Reno from 545, 4/6/50. Traded in to EMD 12/23/64 on GP35.

5461 #1898-12/43 A Reno from 546, 1/27/50. Traded in to EMD 12/26/62 on GP30.

5462 #1910-12/43 B Reno from 546, 1/27/50. Traded in to EMD 4/24/64 on GP35.

5463 #1911-12/43 B Reno from 546, 1/27/50. Traded in to EMD 1/11/65 on GP35.

5464 #1899-12/43 A Reno from 546, 1/27/50. Traded in to EMD 2/24/64 on GP35.

5471 #1900-12/43A Reno from 547, 2/6/50. Traded in to EMD 3/27/62 on GP30.

5472 #1912-12/43 B Reno from 547, 2/6/50. Traded in to EMD 12/23/64 on GP35.

5473 #1913-12/43 B Reno from 547, 2/6/50. Traded in to EMD 3/27/62 on GP30.

5474 #1901-12/43 A Reno from 547, 2/6/50. Traded in to EMD 3/27/62 on GP30.

5481 #1902-3/44 A Reno from 548, 1/10/50. Wrecked, Gore, Colo., 12/5/50; Reblt 3/51 by EMD as 1500 hp F7-1. Traded in to EMD 12/23/64 on GP35.

5482 #1914-3/44 B Reno from 548, 1/10/50. Burned, Durham, Colo., 9/21/63; Traded in to EMD 3/10/64 on GP35.

5483 #1915-3/44 B Reno from 548, 1/11/50. Traded in to EMD 12/23/64 on GP35.

5484 #1903-3/44 A Reno from 548, 1/11/50. Traded in to EMD 3/10/64 on GP35.

5491 #2771-8/44 A Reno from 549, 2/24/50. Traded in to EMD 2/23/62 on GP30.

5492 #2777-8/44 B Reno from 549, 2/24/50. Traded in to EMD 2/23/62 on GP30.

5493 #2778-8/44 B Reno from 549, 2/24/50. Traded in to EMD 2/23/62 on GP30.

5494 #2772-8/44 A Reno from 549, 2/24/50. Traded in to EMD 2/23/62 on GP30.

5501 #2773-8/44 A Reno from 550, 1/31/50. Traded in to EMD 12/3/62 on GP30.

5502 #2779-8/44 B Reno from 550, 1/31/50. Traded in to EMD 12/3/62 on GP30.

5503 #2780-8/44 B Reno from 550, 1/31/50. Traded in to EMD 12/3/62 on GP30.

5504 #2774-8/44 A Reno from 550, 1/31/50. Traded in to EMD 12/3/62 on GP30.

5511 #2775-10/44 A Reno from 551, 2/7/50. Traded in to EMD 12/7/62 on GP30.

5512 #2781-10/44 B Reno from 551, 2/7/50. Traded in to EMD 12/7/62 on GP30.

5513 #2782-10/44 B Reno from 551, 2/7/50. Traded in to EMD 12/7/62 on GP30.

5514 #2776-10/44 A Reno from 551, 2/7/50. Traded in to EMD 12/7/62 on GP30.

Note 1: Gear ratio and weights are after 1953 modification.

Note 2: Units 5482 and 5483 were equipped with steam generators from the time they were delivered. Steam generators were added to units 5492-5493, 5502-5503 and 5512-5513 in March 1948; they were removed in 1953 when the units were regeared.

FT's 5484-5483 were regularly assigned to the overnight Denver-Salt Lake City Prospector *for many years. The F3B was added west of Grand Junction where the train was combined with the* Royal Gorge. (*D&RGW photo—Michael B. Davis Collection*)

F3 6000 hp (1500 hp per unit)

B-B EMD DE B-B 58 62:15[1] 964,940# 241,235# TE[1]

5521 #3544-11/46 A Reno from 552, 1/30/50. Wrecked, Pactolus, Colo., 7/25/65; Traded in to EMD 1/11/66 on GP40.

5522 #3550-11/46 B Reno from 552, 1/30/50. Wrecked, Pactolus, Colo., 7/25/65; Traded in to EMD 1/11/66 on GP40.

5523 #3551-11/46 B Reno from 552, 1/30/50. Wrecked, Pactolus, Colo., 7/25/65; Traded in to EMD 1/11/66 on GP40.

5524 #3545-11/46 A Reno from 552, 1/30/50. Wrecked, Pactolus, Colo., 7/25/65; Traded in to EMD 1/11/66 on GP40.

5531 #3546-11/46 A Reno from 553, 4/12/50. Wrecked, Dos, Colo., 11/20/53; Reblt 2/54 by EMD to 1500 hp F9-A. Traded in to EMD 1/11/66 on GP40.

5532 #3552-11/46 B Reno from 553, 4/12/50. Traded in to EMD 1/11/66 on GP40.

5533 #3553-11/46 B Reno from 553, 4/12/50. Traded in to EMD 1/11/66 on GP40.

5534 #3547-11/46 A Reno from 553, 4/12/50. Traded in to EMD 1/11/66 on GP40.

5541 #3548-11/46 A Reno from 554, 3/6/50. Traded in to EMD 12/2/65 on GP40.

5542 #3554-11/46 B Reno from 554, 3/7/50. Traded in to EMD 12/8/65 on GP40.

5543 #3555-11/46 B Reno from 554, 3/6/50. Traded in to EMD 1/11/66 on GP40.

5544 #3549-11/46 A Reno from 554, 3/6/50. Traded in to EMD 12/8/65 on GP40.

Note 1: Units 5521-5544 originally geared 61:16, with tractive effort of 232,355#.

Note 2: Units 5522-5523, 5532-5533 and 5543-5544 equipped with steam generators.

F7 6000 hp (1500 hp per unit)

B-B	*EMD*	*DE B-B 59*	*62:15*	*976,960# (5551-5574)*	*235,350# TE*
		DE B-B 60	*62:15*	*997,900# (5581-5584)*	*241,440# TE*
		DE B-B 60	*62:15*	*985,850# (5591-5644)*	*241,138# TE*
		DE B-B 59	*62:15*	*973,660# (5651-5694)*	*237,630# TE*
		DE B-B 60	*62:15*	*976,052# (5701-5754)*	*238,220# TE*

5551 #5862-2/49 A Reno from 555, 2/2/50. Traded in to EMD 1/17/68 on SD45.

5552 #5868-2/49 B Reno from 555, 2/2/50. Wrecked, 8/56; Reblt 1/57 by EMD. Sold 5/17/70 to Alaska RR 1517.

5553 #5869-2/49 B Reno from 555, 2/2/50. Wrecked, 8/56; Reblt 8/56 by EMD. Traded in to EMD, 10/8/71 on GP40.

5554 #5863-2/49 A Reno from 555, 2/2/50. Traded in to EMD 1/19/68 on SD45.

5561 #5864-11/48 A Reno from 556, 2/15/50. Wrecked, Mill Fork, Utah, 12/19/63. Traded in to EMD 1/16/68 on SD45. See Note 2.

5562 #5870-11/48 B Reno from 556, 2/15/50. Traded in to EMD 1/16/68 on SD45. See Note 2.

5563 #5871-11/48 B Reno from 556, 2/15/50. Traded in to EMD 1/16/68 on SD45. See Note 2.

5564 #5865-11/48 A Reno from 556, 2/15/50. Traded in to EMD 1/16/68 on SD45. See Note 2.

5571	#5866-2/49	A	Reno from 557, 2/14/50. Wrecked, Dos, Colo., 11/20/53; Reblt 2/54 by EMD to 1500 hp F9-A. Sold 5/17/70 to Alaska RR 1524.
5572	#5872-2/49	B	Reno from 557, 2/14/50. Traded in to EMD 1/17/68 on SD45.
5573	#5873-2/49	B	Reno from 557, 2/14/50. Traded in to EMD 2/20/72 on GP40-2.
5574	#5867-2/49	A	Reno from 557, 2/14/50. Traded in to EMD 2/20/72 on GP40-2.
5581	#8345-5/49	A	Reno from 558, 1/23/50. Traded in to EMD 1/17/68 on SD45.
5582	#8359-5/49	B	Reno from 558, 1/23/50. Traded in to EMD 1/19/68 on SD45.
5583	#8360-5/49	B	Reno from 558, 1/23/50. Traded in to EMD 1/19/68 on SD45.
5584	#8346-5/49	A	Reno from 558, 1/23/50. Traded in to EMD 1/17/68 on SD45.
5591	#8347-7/49	A	Reno from 559, 4/12/50. Wrecked, 7/64; Reblt by EMD, 1/65. Traded in to EMD 2/22/67 on GP40.
5592	#8361-7/49	B	Reno from 559, 4/12/50. Traded in to EMD 2/22/67 on GP40.
5593	#8362-7/49	B	Reno from 559, 4/12/50. Traded in to EMD 12/20/66 on SD45.
5594	#8348-7/49	A	Reno from 559, 4/12/50. Traded in to EMD 2/22/67 on GP40.
5601	#8349-7/49	A	Reno from 560, 4/14/50. Traded in to EMD 7/26/66 on GP40.
5602	#8363-7/49	B	Reno from 560, 4/14/50. Traded in to EMD 2/21/67 on GP40.
5603	#8364-7/49	B	Reno from 560, 4/14/50. Traded in to EMD 3/1/67 on GP40.
5604	#8350-7/49	A	Reno from 560, 4/14/50. Traded in to EMD 3/1/67 on GP40.
5611	#8351-7/49	A	Reno from 561, 2/21/50. Traded in to EMD 3/1/67 on GP40.
5612	#8365-7/49	B	Reno from 561, 2/21/50. Traded in to EMD 7/26/66 on GP40.
5613	#8366-7/49	B	Reno from 561, 2/21/50. Traded in to EMD 3/1/67 on GP40.
5614	#8352-7/49	A	Reno from 561, 2/21/50. Traded in to EMD 12/20/66 on SD45.
5621	#8353-7/49	A	Reno from 562, 2/3/50. Traded in to EMD 7/26/66 on GP40.
5622	#8367-7/49	B	Reno from 562, 2/3/50. Traded in to EMD 3/1/67 on GP40.
5623	#8368-7/49	B	Reno from 562, 2/3/50. Traded in to EMD 7/26/66 on GP40.
5624	#8354-7/49	A	Reno from 562, 2/3/50. Traded in to EMD 2/26/67 on GP40.
5631	#8355-7/49	A	Reno from 563, 2/13/50. Traded in to EMD 5/14/69 on GP40.
5632	#8369-7/49	B	Reno from 563, 2/13/50. Traded in to EMD 1/16/68 on SD45.
5633	#8370-7/49	B	Reno from 563, 2/13/50. Traded in to EMD 1/16/68 on SD45.
5634	#8356-7/49	A	Reno from 563, 2/13/50. Traded in to EMD 1/16/68 on SD45.
5641	#8357-7/49	A	Reno from 564, 4/24/50. Sold 2/22/70 to PC for trade-in to EMD.
5642	#8371-7/49	B	Reno from 564, 4/24/50. Sold 2/22/70 to PC for trade-in to EMD.
5643	#8372-7/49	B	Reno from 564, 4/24/50. Wrecked, Sylvan, Colo., 12/9/56; Reblt 3/57 by EMD. Traded in to EMD 5/12/69 on GP40.
5644	#8358-7/49	A	Reno from 564, 4/24/50. Wrecked, Sylvan, Colo., 12/9/56; Reblt 3/57 by EMD. Sold 8/27/69 to American Crystal Sugar 64, Rocky Ford, Colo. Sold 1980 to Chicago Madison & Northern #564.

5651	#11405-6/50	A	Traded in to EMD 2/22/67 on GP40.
5652	#11415-6/50	B	Traded in to EMD 3/1/67 on GP40.
5653	#11416-6/50	B	Sold 5/15/70 to Alaska RR 1525.
5654	#11406-6/50	A	Sold 5/15/70 to Alaska RR 1530.
5661	#11407-6/50	A	Wrecked, Mill Fork, Utah, 12/19/63; Traded in to EMD 1/16/64 on GP35.
5662	#11417-6/50	B	Sold 2/22/70 to PC for trade-in to EMD.
5663	#11418-6/50	B	Sold 2/22/70 to PC for trade-in to EMD.
5664	#11408-6/50	A	Sold 5/15/70 to Alaska RR 1532.
5671	#11409-6/50	A	Sold for scrap 7/20/67 to Precision Engineering Co., Mt. Vernon, Ill.; Resold to L&N for parts.
5672	#11419-6/50	B	Traded in to EMD 5/14/69 on GP40.
5673	#11420-6/50	B	Sold 2/22/70 to PC for trade-in to EMD.
5674	#11410-6/50	A	Traded in to EMD 5/14/69 on GP40.
5681	#11411-6/50	A	Traded in to EMD 1/16/68 on SD45.
5682	#11421-6/50	B	Traded in to EMD 7/26/66 on GP40.
5683	#11422-6/50	B	Sold for scrap 7/20/67 to Precision Engineering Co., Mt. Vernon, Ill.; Resold 8/67 to TP-MP Term. RR 848B.
5684	#11412-6/50	A	Sold for scrap 7/20/67 to Precision Engineering Co., Mt. Vernon, Ill.; Resold 8/67 to TP-MP Term. RR 848A.
5691	#11413-6/50	A	Sold 2/22/70 to PC for trade-in to EMD.
5692	#11423-6/50	B	Traded in to EMD 5/14/69 on GP40.
5693	#11424-6/50	B	Sold for scrap 7/20/67 to Precision Engineering Co., Mt. Vernon, Ill.; Resold 8/67 to TP-MP Term. RR 849B.
5694	#11414-6/50	A	Sold for scrap 7/20/67 to Precision Engineering Co., Mt. Vernon, Ill.; Resold 8/67 to TP-MP term. RR 849A.
5701	#16517-6/52	A	Wrecked, Mill Fork, Utah, 12/19/63; Traded in to EMD 1/16/64 on GP35.
5702	#16531-6/52	B	Traded in to EMD 11/20/71 on GP40.
5703	#16532-6/52	B	Traded in to EMD 11/20/71 on GP40.
5704	#16518-6/52	A	Traded in to EMD 3/19/72 on GP40-2.
5711	#16519-6/52	A	Sold 5/16/70 to Alaska RR 1520.
5712	#16533-6/52	B	Sold 2/22/70 to PC for trade-in to EMD. Became PC 712; Reno PC 3478; Reno Conrail 3872.
5713	#16534-6/52	B	Traded in to EMD 11/10/71 on GP40.
5714	#16520-6/52	A	Sold 5/16/70 to Alaska RR 1528.
5721	#16521-6/52	A	Sold 2/22/70 to PC for trade-in to EMD. Became PC 721; Reno PC 1878; Reno Conrail 1878.
5722	#16535-6/52	B	Traded in to EMD 10/8/71 on GP40.
5723	#16536-6/52	B	Traded in to EMD 11/10/71 on GP40.
5724	#16522-6/52	A	Sold 5/17/70 to Alaska RR 1526.
5731	#16523-6/52	A	Traded in to EMD 3/19/72 on GP40-2.
5732	#16537-6/52	B	Sold 5/16/70 to Alaska RR 1519.
5733	#16538-6/52	B	Sold 2/22/70 to PC for trade-in to EMD. Became PC 733; Reno PC 3479; Reno Conrail 3873.
5734	#16524-6/52	A	Traded in to EMD 2/26/72 on GP40-2.
5741	#16525-6/52	A	Traded in to EMD 11/20/71 on GP40.
5742	#16539-6/52	B	Traded in to EMD 5/3/72 on GP40-2.
5743	#16540-6/52	B	Sold 5/17/70 to Alaska RR 1521.
5744	#16526-6/52	A	Sold 5/18/70 to Alaska RR 1522.
5751	#16527-7/52	A	Wrecked, Helper, Utah, 1967; Traded in to EMD 1/19/68 on SD45.

5752	#16541-7/52	B	Traded in to EMD 11/20/71 on GP40.
5753 (2nd)	#16542-7/52	B	Reno from 5762 (1st), 11/24/55.[1] Sold 5/18/70 to Alaska RR 1523.
5754	#16528-7/52	A	Sold 2/22/70 to PC for trade-in to EMD. Became PC 754; Reno PC 1879; Reno Conrail 1879.
5761	#16529-7/52	A	Traded in to EMD 3/31/72 on GP40-2.
5762 (2nd)	#20531-9/55	B	1750 hp F9-B. Reno from 5753 (1st), 11/24/55.[1] In service, 1983.
5763	#20532-9/55	B	1750 hp F9-B. In service, 1983.
5764	#16530-7/52	A	Traded in to EMD 3/31/72 on GP40-2.

Note 1: Units 5751/5752/5754 and 5761/5762(1st)/5764 were delivered as A/B/A sets. In Sept. 1955, F9-Bs 5753(1st) and 5763 were delivered, making 5751-5754 and 5761-5764 into F7-A/F7-B/F9-B/F7-A sets. In Nov. 1955, two of the B-units traded sets and were renumbered, making 5751-5754 a pure F7 A/B/B/A set and 5761-5764 an F7-A/F9-B/F9-B/F7-A set. This latter set had 6500 hp, weighed 991,100# and exerted a tractive effort of 238,320#.

Note 2: EMD refers to these units as F5.

Note 3: Units 5552, 5553, 5562, 5563, 5571-5574, 5762 (2nd) and 5763 originally equipped with steam generators. They were added to 5582, 5583, and steam generator cars 250 and 251 when removed from FT B units 5492-5513 in 1953.

F3's 5521-5522-5523-5524 were regularly used on to the California Zephyr for more than a decade. Here they ease No. 17 onto Rio Grande rails at Prospect Junction, Denver, at the beginning of its 13½-hour journey to Salt Lake City; on March 25, 1951. More unusual is the view below of F7 5684 with four companions and ex-Alco PB1 steam generator 253 leading a twenty car eastbound Illini Railroad Club Special through Canon City on June 18, 1966. (Above, Richard H. Kindig photo; below, Ed Fulcomer Collection)

F9 7000 hp (1750 hp per unit)

B-B EMD DE B-B 60 62:15 990,820# 238,290# TE

5771 #20527-9/55 A In service, 1983

5772 #20529-9/55 B Wrecked, Grizzly, Colo., 7/25/65; Traded in to EMD 9/14/65 on GP40.

5773 #20530-9/55 B Wrecked, Grizzly, Colo., 3/29/68; Sold for scrap 5/69 to Precision Engineering Co., Mt. Vernon, Ill.

5774 #20528-9/55 A Wrecked, Grizzly, Colo., 3/29/68; Sold for scrap 5/69 to Precision Engineering Co., Mt. Vernon, Ill.

Units 5772 and 5773 equipped with steam generators. See also units 5762(2nd) and 5763.

GP9 1750 hp

B-B EMD DE B-B 60 (5901-5924) DE B-B 61 (5931-5954) 62:15 245,646# (5901-5924) 250,180# (5931-5954) 60,019# TE 60,770# TE

5901 #20515-5/55 Traded in to EMD 2/20/72 on GP40-2.

5902 #20516-5/55

5903 #20517-5/55

5904 #20518-5/55

5911 #20519-5/55

5912 #20520-5/55 Leased to Carbon County RR, 4/28/58 to 5/24/58.

5913 #20521-5/55

5914 #20522-5/55

5921 #20523-5/55

5922 #20524-5/55

5923 #20525-6/55 Sold 1/77 to Utah Power & Light Co., Castle Gate, Utah.

5924 #20526-6/55

5931 #22068-7/56

5932 #22069-7/56

5933 #22070-8/56 Wrecked, Crater, Colo., 7/19/75; Sold 5/10/77 to Itel Equipment Management Co.; Resold 6/77 to Illinois Central Gulf and reblt as ICG 8203.

5934 #22071-7/56

5941 #22072-7/56

5942 #22073-7/56 Damaged, Monarch Branch, 9/16/69; Reblt by EMD.

5943 #22074-7/56 Damaged, Monarch Branch, 9/16/69; Reblt by EMD. Wrecked, Salt Lake City, 4/19/76; Sold 5/18/77 to Itel Equipment Management Co.; Resold 6/77 to Illinois Central Gulf and reblt as ICG 8323.

5944 #22075-7/56

5951 #22076-7/56

5952 #22077-7/56

5953 #22078-7/56

5954 #22079-7/56

The GP9's have served the Rio Grande well in many capacities for a quarter century. There is barely room on No. 5904's flank for the new style "Rio Grande". (Thomas Lyons)

F9A 5771, destined to become famous as the D&RGW's last "covered wagon" A-unit, leads four mates into Helper, Utah, on September 15, 1968, with the eastbound California Zephyr. Three extra cars have put all 8250 HP to good use over Soldier Summit. (Ed Fulcomer)

PA1/PB1 6000 hp (2000 hp per unit)

A1A-A1A ALCO DE A1A-A1A 49 64:19 919,980#1 147,792# TE[1]

6001	#74684-1/47	A	Reno from 600A, 3/13/50. Sold for scrap 7/20/67 to Precision Engineering Co., Mt. Vernon, Ill.
6002	#74702-2/47	B	Reno from 600B, 3/31/50. Ret 8/16/65; Conv to Steam Generator Car 253, 10/65.
6003	#74685-2/47	A	Reno from 600C, 3/13/50. Sold for scrap 7/20/67 to Precision Engineering Co., Mt. Vernon, Ill.
6011	#74686-4/47	A	Reno from 601A, 3/6/50. Traded in to EMD 12/20/67 on SD45.
6012	#74703-4/47	B	Reno from 601B, 3/6/50. Ret 5/10/65; Conv. to Steam Generator Car 252, 7/65.
6013	#74687-4/47	A	Reno from 601C, 3/6/50. Sold for scrap 7/20/67 to Precision Engineering Co., Mt. Vernon, Ill.

Note 1: Weight and tractive effort shown for A/B/A set. Extra water capacity was added to each unit in 10/48.

Units 6001-6013 equipped with steam generators.

The last local passenger service on the Rio Grande was provided by Nos. 9 & 10, on the old Moffat run to Craig. These trains were also the last stand for the Alco PA's and the 6003 is seen eastbound at Phippsburg in 1967. (Ed Fulcomer) An earlier effort in branch line service is represented by Motor Car No. 592, a converted combine used briefly prior to 1930 on the Leadville and Creede branches. Here it is stored in Denver in 1938. It had been built by Pullman in May 1898 as Rio Grande Western coach No. 216, was renumbered D&RG 784 in 1909 and rebuilt as a combine in 1920. The two 100 HP six cylinder Continental engines were removed in November 1938 and the car was used for several years on the Aspen Branch mixed. Finally retired in 1951, its body was sold to T. M. Steele of Denver. (Otto Perry, Denver Public Library Western History Collection)

The Prospector

Motor Train No. 2 rests in the Burnham coach yard after being towed in by a reliable "iron horse", an embarrassingly frequent circumstance for the little train. However, No. 1 (below) is under its own power on the home stretch into Denver Union Station on Sunday morning, December 7, 1941. (both, John W. Maxwell)

The D&RGW's entry into the world of lightweight, stainless steel, diesel powered passenger service was made on November 17, 1941 with these two diminutive Budd-built trains, the first Prospector. Originated by Judge Wilson McCarthy, receiver and later president of the railroad, they managed to squeeze four 192 HP six cylinder Hercules engines, baggage compartment, 44 coach seats, dressing rooms, eight sections, two roomettes, kitchen, dining and lounge space into their 153-foot lengths. Unfortunately, the pair proved unequal to their demanding schedule, as well as having too much coach and too little Pullman space, and the exingencies of war brought a premature end to the trains in July 1942, after less than nine months in service. They were returned to Budd and subsequently scrapped.

D&RGWRR
ROYAL GORGE ROUTE
SCENIC LINE

(Top) F3A 554A awaits departure from Denver in 1947 with the postwar heavyweight Prospector. *(Otto Perry, Denver Public Library Western History Collection)*

Narrow gauge steam power was still plentiful at Alamosa in the 1950's. (above, Museum Collection) The major diesel repair shop is at Burnham where the Denver & Rio Grande was born over a century ago. (both, John E. Tudek)

The speed with which time can eliminate once common scenes is demonstrated by these photos of not too many years ago – a 1500 taking water at Palmer Lake, F units on a passenger train passing an RS3, the final run on the Sapinero branch and an Alco with the vestiges of the Royal Gorge at Pueblo. One day, a picture of an SD40T-2 will be just as nostalgic. (below, Ross Grenard; right, Museum Collection; center right, Robert W. Richardson; bottom, Ed Fulcomer)

DENVER & RIO GRANDE WESTERN RAILROAD
• SCENIC LINE OF THE WORLD •

(Above) The four month old California Zephyr *eases out of Denver Union Station behind Alco A-B-A set No. 601 in fresh silver paint and with a commendable lack of the usual Alco black exhaust. (Ross Grenard) These units were first painted in the traditional black and yellow, as the 600 with the* Exposition Flyer *at Utah Junction in 1948. (Richard H. Kindig photo, Ed Fulcomer Collection)*

(Right) The engineer of M-67 class 4-8-2 No. 1530 tinkers with his engine's left side rod assembly as he awaits a call for helper service at Buena Vista, Colorado, in February 1941. (John W. Maxwell) Old man winter applied a streamlined casing to the boiler of No. 483 at Cumbres Pass, in a gesture probably not appreciated by the crew. (Robert W. Richardson)

Baldwin compound C-41 No. 1105 became K-37 narrow gauge 2-8-2 No. 493 in 1928. She is still on the roster in 1980, stored at Alamosa. (Museum Collection) Narrow gauge Vauclain compound No. 450 is illustrated below in photo and diagram. Neither the compound cylinders nor the slopeback tender lasted long. (Horace W. Curtis photo, John W. Maxwell Collection)

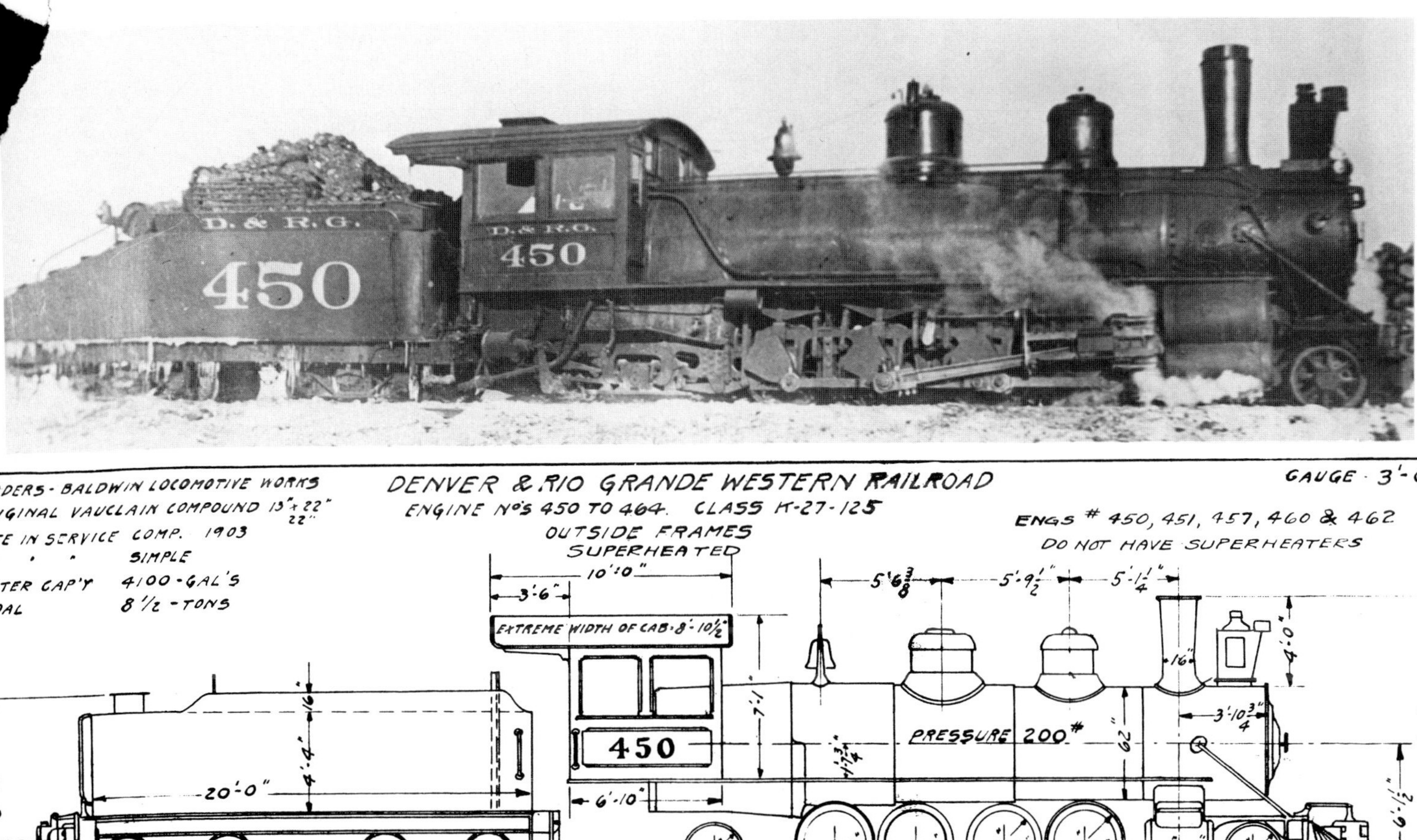

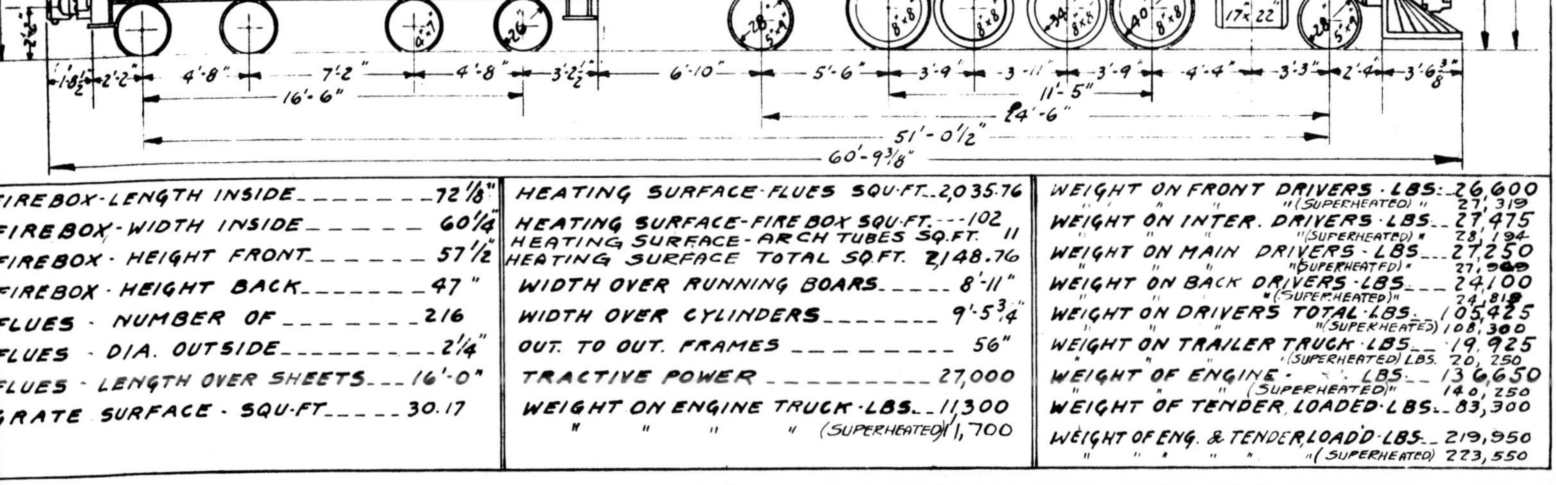

DENVER & RIO GRANDE WESTERN R.R.

4000 HP 165 TON DIESEL HYDRAULIC FREIGHT LOCOMOTIVE (ML-4) CLASS DH C-C 1
4001, 4002, 4003

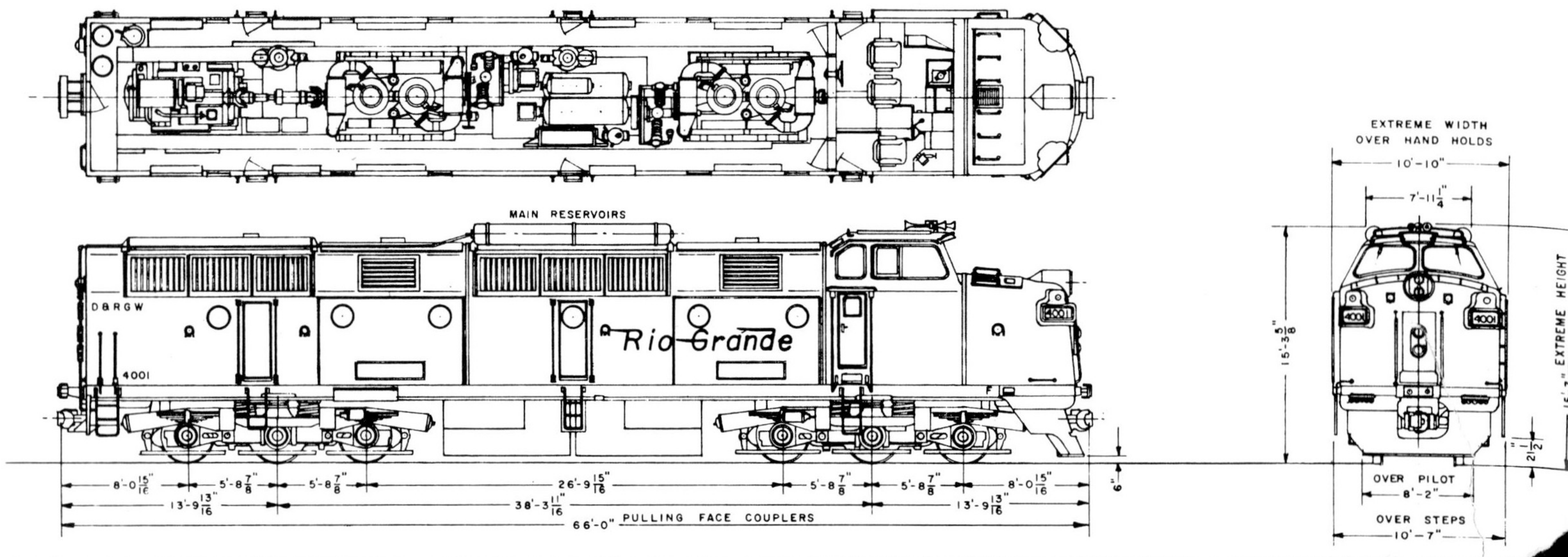

MINIMUM CURVE RADIUS _ _ _ _ _ _ _ (23°) 250 FT.
MAXIMUM SPEED _ _ _ _ _ _ _ 70 MPH
TRACTIVE EFFORT WITH ½ VARIABLE SUPPLIES _ _ _ 104,080 LBS.

COUPLERS _ _ _ _ _ _ _ AAR TYPE E
DRAFT GEAR _ _ _ _ _ _ _ NATIONAL MALLEABLE TYPE M-380
WHEELS _ _ _ _ _ _ _ 40" DIA.
JOURNALS _ _ _ _ _ _ _ SKF SPHERICAL ROLLER - 223 34 C/C 3

CAB HEATER AND DEFROSTER _ _ _ _ _ _ _ KLIMATOR - TYPE 2016

AIR BRAKES _ _ _ _ _ _ _ WESTINGHOUS
TRUCK BRAKES _ _ _ _ _ _ _ CLAS

ENGINES TWO 16 CYL. EACH LOCO. _ _ _ _ _ MAYBACH M
ENGINE RATING _ _ _ _ _ _ _ 2,00
STARTER MOTOR AND GENERATOR _ _ _ _ _ _ _ BROWN - BOV
EXHAUST TURBOCHARGER _ _ _ _ _ _ _ MAYBACH AGL-
HYDRAULIC TRANSMISSION _ _ _ _ _ _ _ VOITH L8-30 R

COOLING WATER PREHEATER _ _ _ _ _ _ _ HAGENUK 593

GEAR TRAIN _ _ _ _ _ _ _ MAYBACH 870-1

BATTERIES - NIFE TYPE 7-RDT 25032, 64 VOLTS, 385 AMPERE HOURS
HEADLIGHTS _ _ _ _ _ _ _ 1 - TWIN SEALED AND 1 - MARS

SPEED RECORDER _ _ _ _ _ _ _ CHICAGO PNEUMATIC

FUEL OIL _ _ _ _ _ _ _ 3,200 GALS.
LUBRICATING OIL _ _ EACH ENGINE - 116 GALS., LOCO. - 232 GALS.
HYDRAULIC OIL - EACH TRANSMISSION - 170 GALS., LOCO. - 340 GALS.

COOLING SYSTEM _ _ _ EACH ENGINE - 436 GALS., LOCO. - 872 GALS.
WATER SPRAY SYSTEM _ _ _ _ _ _ _ 200 GALS.
SAND _ _ _ _ _ _ _ 44 CU. FT.) 4,410 LBS.

WEIGHT ON NO. 1 TRUCK (LOADED) AV. _ _ _ _ _ _ _ 162,804 LBS
WEIGHT ON NO. 2 TRUCK (LOADED) AV. _ _ _ _ _ _ _ 167,523 LBS

TOTAL LIGHT WEIGHT (DRY) AV. _ _ _ _ _ _ _ 289,697 LBS
TOTAL WEIGHT WITH ONE-HALF VARIABLE SUPPLIES _ _ 315,427 LBS
TOTAL LOADED WEIGHT ON RAIL, AV. _ _ _ _ _ _ _ 330,327 LBS

AIR COMPRESSORS _ _ _ _ _ _ TWO WESTINGHOUSE TYPE 3-CDCB

CONTROL EQUIPMENT _ _ _ _ _ _ _ ELECTRO - PNEUMATIC

BUILDERS _ _ KRAUSS - MAFFEI, MUNCHEN, GERMANY.
DATE IN SERVICE _ _ _ NOV., 1961.

All three of the KM diesel-hydraulics, 4003-4002-4001, roll dynamometer car 10 and a 95-car freight down the two percent grade past the old Rollinsville ice house in June 1962. Notwithstanding their rugged appearance, these units did not prove to offer any significant improvement over diesel-electrics, and the experiment was given up in less than two years. (Otto C. Perry, Denver Public Library Western History Collection)

Unusual Steam Locomotive Assignment Problems

By Robert W. Richardson

Railroads generally as they received newer and heavier locomotives would gradually retire older and lighter classes to use as helpers, switchers or for replacing even lighter power on branches. In this practice the D&RG/D&RGW was similar to other companies in respect to its standard gauge lines. At the end of standard gauge steam(1956) the road was using mostly its 1100-series 1906 2-8-0s on branches and for switchers, with a few 3600-series articulateds lasting to that final year as helpers. All other steam was gone.

But the Rio Grande had one important difference: hundreds of miles of narrow gauge and after the turn of the century, very little of it was three -rail trackage. The standard gauge lines, often converted from the original narrow gauge, received the new locomotives and cars as management concentrated its often meager funds on the standard gauge. The narrow gauge was given retired items such as rail, bridges and turntables, but of course could not use the older standard gauge rolling stock.

The result was for the narrow gauge to keep on rebuilding very old engines. These were given new boilers, new tenders and modern appurtenances, but in general they remained little changed in appearance or usefulness from when they were new in the 1880s.

Again, for lack of funds, some portions of the narrow gauge remained to the end with light rails and light bridges. Changing these had low priority. Again and again, plans to upgrade were at the bottom of the list, seldom and sometimes never done.

Until the end of operations in the Gunnison area the Baldwin Branch was an example of "never." The bridge over the Slate River was on the upgrading intentions for years, but the work was never done, so only C-16 Class engines could run on it. That is why 1882 relics #268 and #278 remained at Gunnison so long — the 268 until abandonment.

Similarly, the line through the Black Canyon beyond Sapinero to Cimarron would permit nothing larger than a C-21 Class, though "mudhens" (K-27) could be moved dead. The latter had clearance on bridges down to inches, and regular operation was too risky.

Until arrival in 1925 of the K-36 mikados, engines such as C-16, C-19 and C-21 worked as helpers with the K-27 and K-28 Classes on Marshall Pass, a not very efficient arrangement. The mikados had a "gait" (about 14 mph) at which they were most efficient on the 4% grades, but the smaller engines had better efficiency at several miles-per-hour less.

The arrival of the 490 series in 1928-30 ended much of the need for 2-8-0 types, as the K-37s released other mikados for use where 2-8-0 types held sway. The K-37s were so successful that management had on the drawing boards some mallets to be built from other old standard gauge 2-8-0s. The Depression ended those plans.

The 1880s narrow gauge 4-6-0s on passenger runs were gradually ousted from much of that service by the arrival in 1923 of the K-28 mikados numbered in the 470s. A few 4-6-0s remained in use on the Chili Line and the main line west of Gunnison due mainly to light rail. In the 1930s the Chili Line received heavier rail and the passenger train west of Gunnison was discontinued, ending all need of the 4-6-0s. The K-28 types took over many of the passenger and freight runs west of Alamosa, handling most of the passenger runs until those were discontinued in 1951.

Last stand of the mudhens was at Durango. They handled the Silverton runs and also the varying needs of the Rio Grande Southern until that line quit in 1951. Between 1925 and 1927 the RGS was upgraded so as to be able to use the mudhens, now surplus from the main lines over Cumbres and Marshall passes.

In turn the RGS's own C-16s were sent to storage and eventual scrap as the entire C-19 Class became available in 1925, where it remained until the road was ready for the mudhens. So by the mid-1920s both roads had replaced most of the C-16 Class, to the extent that it nearly vanished. Gradually the C-18s and C-19s followed.

The C-18s were purchased in World War I and assigned almost entirely for years west of Gunnison to Ouray. To the end of the Ouray Branch in 1953 this was true. Mudhens could be used between Cimarron and Ridgway, but this came to an end with abandonment of the line through the canyon in 1949 and the end of the RGS.

Narrow gauge engines were used for years to switch dual gauge yards, especially those at Salida and Montrose. At Montrose, an idler car was used to switch standard gauge cars, even to wye the standard gauge *Mountaineer*. At Salida a narrow gauge 2-8-0 could often be found in use in the 1930s and also the only mikado equipped with dual-gauge couplers, the 496. Alamosa used mikados sparingly and in final decades only in emergency shortages of switch engines with a K-36 using an idler, for example. The final remaining stretch of main line three-rail track (Alamosa to Antonito) for much of the year saw only narrow gauge engines handling mixed gauge freights. Idler cars were used to couple between the two gauges, both in the train and in switching. During one Cumbres snow blockade, when all narrow gauge power was busy with that problem, the last mixed-gauge passenger train was operated, using several narrow gauge cars powered by standard gauge 2-8-0 #1146, which was equipped with dual couplers and thus did not need to use an idler car for the round trip to Antonito from Alamosa.

LOCOMOTIVE CLASSIFICATIONS

The original system was based on the engine weight. For example, the 60 Class weighed approximately 60,000 pounds. No indication of wheel arrangement was made. In 1923 a new system was adopted with a letter to designate wheel arrangement, followed by a number stating tractive effort to the nearest 1000 pounds. The letter M was used for both 4-8-2s and 4-8-4s. All articulateds were given letter L. Until the end of steam operation the railroad continued to use the old system in its summaries of equipment as the "Motive Power Class" and the new system as the "Road Class". However, the only additional locomotives to receive both designations were the K-36(189) and M-75(419) types in 1925 and 1926, and all power purchased after this was identified by the road class only.

CLASS CHANGE OF 1923

NARROW GAUGE

Old	New	Old	New
47	T-12	72	C-18
60	C-16	93	C-21
70	C-19	112	C-25
71	C-17	125	K-27
		140	K-28

STANDARD GAUGE

Old	*New*	*Old*	*New*
65	C-14	180	C-42
75	S-19	183	C-38
76	T-17	184	T-29
80	C-16	185	C-41
96	S-23	186	C-40
100	G-20	187	C-39
106	T-18	190	C-41
113	C-28	199	C-40
115	T-17	220	C-48
120	C-26	261	P-44
124	Not assigned	280	K-59
		340	L-62
130	T-19	377	M-67
141	G-28	378	M-67
145	T-19	383	M-78
149	S-33	429	F-81
150	T-26	458	L-96
154	G-28	532	L-107
161	T-24		
170	T-28		
172	C-39		
175	T-31		

RGS41 at Dolores in 1947 is fitted with one of the large steel plows that were used on many narrow gauge D&RGW engines as well. These remained on year around, being useful against rocks as well as snow and were often interchanged during shoppings. The 41 without its plow had been photographed at Ridgway in 1940.

No.1034, leaving Denver Union Station with the Craig train in 1950, illustrates the D&SL 2-8-0s as they looked in D&RGW dress. (Three photos, Otto Perry, Denver Public Library Western History Collection)

(Top) There was no mistaking FT 551-A which carried its number in no fewer than seven places including a wedge-shaped roof-top indicator that may have been unique to this unit. Freshly painted in a revised scheme, 547 rolls downgrade through Arvada, Colorado in 1947. An ABA lash-up in freight service was unusual on the D&RGW. At the right, dilapidated 458 Class 1062 was at Littleton depot in 1919. Note the white-leaded rods, absence of front number plate, empty headlight box and white flags denoting an extra. (Three photos, Otto Perry, Denver Public Library Western History Collection)

In the pre-dawn hours, two veteran first generation EMD units await their next calls on the servicing tracks at East Yard, Grand Junction in the Fall of 1966. By this date, the 5681 was one of the few covered wagons still wearing the old four stripe paint. (Ed Fulcomer)